Life Lessons

for the Wise

Whispers from the World

A series of engaging short stories, reflections and timeless nuggets to empower your life, mindset, relationships, and growth.

Lawrence Carlos

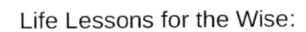

Copyright

Copyright © 2024 **Life Lessons for The Wise: Whispers from the World** by **Lawrence Carlos**

ALL RIGHTS RESERVED. No part of this book may be reproduced, stored in a retrieval system, or transmitted in any form, or by any means, electronic, mechanical, photocopying, recording, or otherwise, without the prior written permission of the author and publisher, except in brief reviews.

All Bible Scriptures are taken from the New King James Version®. Copyright © 1982 by Thomas Nelson. Used by permission. All rights reserved.

Text images in this book were created using Canva.com. All images are used under Canva's standard license terms. Please refer to Canva's Terms of Service for more information at https://www.canva.com/

Connect with the author at:

https://www.facebook.com/LCARLOSMANMAN/

Editing, typesetting, proofreading, graphic and cover design by: Dr Jacqueline N Samuels

https://tinyurl.com/AuthorJNSamuels
ISBN: **9798339147848**

Contents

Copyright	iii
Dedication	vi
Endorsements	viii
Foreword	x
Acknowledgments	xi
Grazing with Stories: A Prologue	xiv
Chapter One: A Good Start in Life	1
Chapter Two: A Leopard Does Not Change Its Spots	5
Chapter Three: Guard Your Words	9
Chapter Four: The Answer to Your Problems	12
Chapter Five: Breach of Trust	17
Chapter Six: Old Habits Die Hard	20
Chapter Seven: Mistaken Identity	22
Chapter Eight: A Wise Man Changes His Mind	24
Chapter Nine: Birds of a Feather Flock Together	32
Chapter Ten: One Man's Meat	39
Chapter Eleven: One Day at A Time	43
Chapter Twelve: From Setback to Success	46
Chapter Thirteen: Look Beyond Behaviours	49
Chapter Fourteen: Denied By Character	57
Chapter Fifteen: Your Skeleton will Come to Life	64
Chapter Sixteen: Do Not Betray Anybody	69
Chapter Seventeen: Don't Compare Yourself to Others	72
Chapter Eighteen: Listen To Your Gut Feeling	76
Chapter Nineteen: Do Not Lose Hope	81

Chapter Twenty: Look At the Bigger Picture	85
Chapter Twenty-One: A Blessing in Disguise	88
Chapter Twenty-Two: By Their Fruits	91
Chapter Twenty-Three: Cheap is Expensive	97
Chapter Twenty-Four: Blame Yourself	101
Chapter Twenty-Five: Nothing Is Worth Dying For	104
Chapter Twenty-Six: Love in Those Days	108
Chapter Twenty-Seven: Not All That Glitters Is Gold	111
Chapter Twenty-Eight: Mistaken Identity Abroad	114
Chapter Twenty-Nine: A Father's Regret	118
Chapter Thirty: Aim High and Seize Opportunities	122
Chapter Thirty-One: Don't Waste Your Chance	125
Chapter Thirty-Two: The Power of Your Tongue	131
Chapter Thirty-Three: Take a Closer Look	135
Chapter Thirty-Four: Stop Being Your Own Enemy	139
Chapter Thirty-Five: Rise Above Your Thinking	143
Chapter Thirty-Six: Remain Calm in Every Situation	146
Chapter Thirty-Seven: Seize the Opportunity	148
Chapter Thirty-Eight: The Power of Giving	152
Chapter Thirty-Nine: The Eleventh Hour	156
Chapter Forty: Tomorrow Will Come	160
Conclusion	164
About the Author	165

Dedication

I dedicate this book to my dear mother *Eunice Wamahiga* who educated us and ensured that we all became successful in our calling. Her endurance, tenacity, faith and positive influence have shaped my character, endurance, hunger for self-improvement, and spiritual connection with God. Among her wisdom nuggets imprinted on my memory are:

You can't gamble. You can't steal. Value education. Read widely. Surround yourself with forward thinking people. Live with integrity.

I thank God for blessing you with unique wisdom and insight to your old age (91 at the time of writing this book). May God continually nourish your life with great health, sound mind and peace. May your children, grandchildren, and great-grandchildren continue to make you proud as each one fulfils their destiny and purpose on earth.

My siblings: Thank you for joining hands with our mother to ensure I received a good education. May your diligent sowing into other people's lives yield a rich harvest as God continues to favour the work of your hands.

Best Mum

Mum, there is none like you, there will never be
On cold mornings you would wake up to pray for us
Through wormy mud and thistles, you disappeared into the darkness
You soldiered on, between thick forests
On steep slippery valleys, you fell, and determinedly stood up
On flooded bridges you walked alone, not afraid of the angry waters
Travelling you had to, for us to see another day -
Mum, there is none like you!

Poisonous snakes, spiders and scorpions filled your path
With your children in mind, you did not care
With robbers and witches hovering around, you did not care
With hunger pangs and falling rain, you moved on
You never gave up
Travelling you had to, for us to see another day -
Mum, there is none like you!

Destination so near, yet so far
From bicycle to motorcycle, from minibus to buses you travelled
Towards sunset, you reached the destination, hungry and tired
You made loses, you made profits, but was determined
With God at the Apex, you prayed for us, we prayed for you
Travelling you had to, for us to see another day -
Mum, there is none like you!

The Force that kept all planets in perfect orbit kept us together
In this world or the next, no evil shall befall you
You would finally return home, glory be to God
The little you made gave us hope to live another day
Your travelling was not in vain, we are because you were
Travelling you had to, for us to see another day -
Mum, there is none like you!

Poem by: ***Lawrence Carlos*** for my mother

Endorsements

I've been reading Lawrence Carlos's stories for a while now, and I'm thrilled that they are finally available in a book. **Life Lessons for the Wise** is a well-written book that anyone eager for life knowledge will appreciate.

— *Mayor Elizabeth Kang'ethe*

While we are alive, we will encounter challenges which can teach us valuable life lessons if we pay attention. That's why I'm grateful to Lawrence Carlos for writing **Life Lessons for the Wise**. I highly recommend this book to anyone seeking to understand life's lessons.

— *Misterseed.com*

Life Lessons for the Wise is a book of short stories that are not only entertaining but also informative. I do not know of anybody who would not laugh after reading the stories but after the laughter is over, one realises that Lawrence Carlos was sharing important experiences and life lessons.

— *Gabriel Gatheru Rwamba*

Director, Match Options Ltd

It is an absolute honour to endorse this incredible book by Mr Lawrence Carlos. Having had the privilege of working with him over six years ago and being part of his vibrant social media community where he shares life-transforming messages, I can truly say his wisdom is unparalleled.

For anyone seeking guidance, whether in parenting, business, or everyday life, this is a must-read book. Its simplicity makes it accessible to all, yet its impact is profound.

I thank God that 'Uncle Lawrence' as I affectionately call him, has finally brought his insights to the pages of this remarkable book **Life Lessons for the Wise: Whispers from the World**. Don't miss out!

— *Reverend Ruth Tiso*

Minister of Pear Tree Road Baptist Church, Derby, UK

Foreword

From the moment I met my husband Lawrence, it was clear that he was a natural storyteller. His captivating tales made me forget that we were meeting for the very first time. Over the years, he has remained the same—endlessly fascinating and full of life lessons.

Lawrence believes that if people truly understood each other, many of the world's problems could be solved. He despises seeing others suffer from issues that could be resolved through open communication. While no one is perfect, he holds that love and understanding are key to happiness. We are here only for a season, and when our time is up, we leave this world for others to inhabit.

In such a rapidly changing world, staying relevant requires continuous learning. Reading allows us to explore an author's mind, gain insight into their experiences, and better grasp the themes of their stories.

Lawrence's stories are shaped by his humble upbringing in Africa and his extensive interactions with diverse people throughout his career. He combined these experiences to write a book focused on making the world a better place.

I wholeheartedly recommend his book, **Life Lessons for the Wise**. I am confident that it will enrich your life.

With much love,

Mrs Mary Carlos

Acknowledgments

While many people have touched my life in various ways. I am indebted to the following:

To *Almighty God my Creator*, thank You for the gifts of life, family, friends and the ability to share Your gifts with the world through these **Life Lessons for the Wise: Whispers from the World**.

I take this opportunity to thank *my mother* for taking me to school where I learned English among other subjects. I am grateful for the countless life lessons you taught me that continue to guide me.

I salute my amazing wife *Mrs Mary Carlos* for your tireless encouragement, inspiration and contribution to this work and your insightful Foreword. I appreciate you.

Thank you my children *Michelle* and *Herman* for your encouragement. Against your wish, you obediently lowered the music volume to accord me peace to write!

To all *my siblings*, you are jewels for your immense contributions that have made me who I am today.

Hats off to *Mr Peter Njiiri Karanja* aka *Misterseed* for giving me the first platform to author my stories and encourage many lives.

I extend my heartfelt thanks to *Councillor Elizabeth Kangethe*, *Mr Gabriel Gatheru Rwamba*. *Misterseed.com* and *Reverend Ruth Tiso* for endorsing my work. Your valuable insights and belief in these life lessons have given me the confidence to share them with a broader audience.

I cannot forget to thank the teachers who taught me English: *Mr Esau Wamugi, Mr Samuel Thige* and *Mrs Kabuthu*, God bless you all for seeing and nurturing my talent.

I thank all those who read my stories and encouraged me to write. I am deeply humbled by your support. Our paths will meet again in other books that are about to be published.

To my editor, graphic designer and publisher *Dr Jacqueline N Samuels*, thank you for publishing my work. You are a publisher every author would be proud to work with.

God bless you all.

Sincerely,

Lawrence Carlos

My Family

As the sun rises, my family is blessed
I have seen the marvels of nature
But never have I seen better people than my family
Remarkable people you are, my First Prize Lottery of life –
You are the best!

As the moon shines, my family is blessed
From toddlers to adults, I have watched you grow
From a girl to a mother, I have watched you grow
Together you all make me smile, you are my greatest hope
Remarkable people you are, my First Prize Lottery of life –
You are the best!

As the stars shine, my family is blessed
Through mountains and valleys, we have travelled
I gave up, you raised me up, I was sad you gave me a smile
How good it is to be alive and call you, 'my family'
Remarkable people you are, my First Prize Lottery of life –
You are the best!

As the Earth revolves around the sun, my family is blessed
May goodness surround you, may happiness shine upon you
Solomonic wisdom will be your trademark
In abundance you will live
The sun, moon and the stars will always shine brightly
You are remarkable people, my First Prize Lottery of life –
YOU ARE THE BEST!

Poem by **Lawrence Carlos** for the family

Grazing with Stories: *A Prologue*

The sun beat down on my back as I herded the cows with my older brothers. They clutched these magical things called library books, their faces buried deep in adventures I couldn't touch. Everyone said my siblings were *bright*, a word that hung over my head like a mystery. All I knew was that their good grades earned them a different kind of treatment and respect.

For some reason, I never went to that place called *Nursery school* where they learned their magic. As a result, I landed straight in Year One, completely lost. The teacher expected everyone to read, write, even sing songs I'd never heard of.

It didn't take him long to discover my blank stare, the empty space where knowledge should be. He'd call me up to the front of the class, open the book like a sacred code, and demand I read aloud. My answer, "I can't", only brought the sting of his whip. It was a confusing, lonely pain. How could my siblings shine so bright, while I was stuck in the shadows?

One Friday, the teacher cornered my eldest brother, Cyrus. His voice laced with disappointment, he referred to my *poor academic ability*. Cyrus, ever the hero, understood the missing piece – *Nursery school*.

That weekend, my world changed. He started with simple things – the alphabet, building words like tiny houses. Numbers followed, a different kind of language.

The teacher had already branded me f*oolish*, shoving me in a group he clearly considered the same. Harsh doesn't even begin to describe it.

But Cyrus wouldn't let that label stick. Every night, before tackling his own work, he'd patiently teach me, giving me practice problems to solve. Slowly, the fog began to clear. My grades started climbing, my hand hesitantly reaching for answers in class. By year's end, I could devour books in our native tongue with ease. The teacher, surprised by the transformation, pulled me out of the *foolish* group and placed me with the *Bests*. Beating, however, remained part of the curriculum – a twisted kind of *integrity test*, he called it.

Meanwhile, my brothers' library books held stories in a language I craved – English. Their laughter, fuelled by these mysterious tales, only amplified my longing. As curiosity gnawed at me, I'd beg them to translate, piece by piece, these fantastical worlds.

One story, about three slumbering ogres, stands out. Each would wake, blame the other for a hit, leading to a hilarious, log-swinging brawl. As a kid, I devoured these stories, praying for the power to unlock them myself.

When Cyrus left for a faraway high school, my mentor was gone. But George, my brilliant older brother, stepped up. He'd test me as he did his own homework, pushing me to reach for something more. With time, English became a familiar friend.

By Year Four, my teacher recognized my newfound fluency. He even entrusted me with a library book, a story I was to share with the entire school.

Standing on that desk, surrounded by eager faces, I became the weaver of words, my voice painting a picture for them all. A simple reward – an exercise book and two pencils – felt like a treasure.

English, as far back as I can remember, has always been my guiding light. Stories are adventures waiting to unfold, each day a new chapter. My teachers, thankfully, have always seen that spark. Even in high school, Mrs Kabuthu, my English teacher, cast me in a play, allowing me to share my gift on stage.

Living abroad, I noticed a troubling disconnect from our roots. So, I started writing stories, using humour to draw people in before gently nudging them to confront societal ills. Since 2005, my stories, shared on a London-based website **www.misterseed.com,** have aimed to change mindsets and spark a transformation.

Now, with God's guidance, I have gratefully connected with inspiring author Reverend Ruth Tiso who introduced me to author and publishing mentor Dr Jacqueline N Samuels. This book, **Life Lessons for the Wise: Whispers from the World**, is the culmination of that journey.

I hope these stories not only educate and inform, but also entertain you. Thank you for joining me on this adventure. May God bless you.

Lawrence Carlos

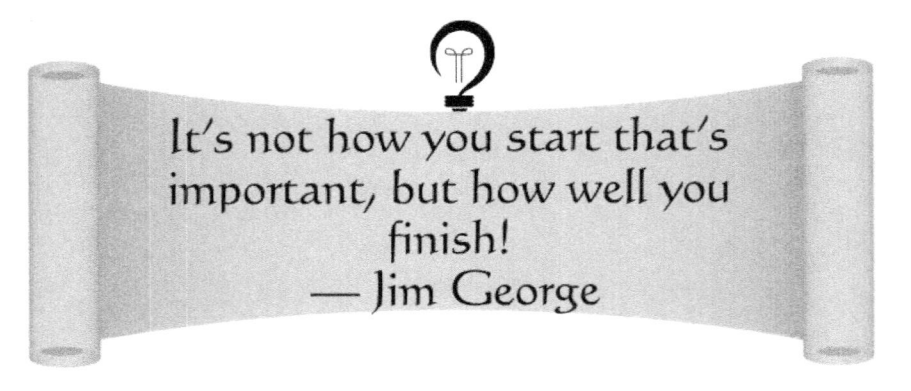

> It's not how you start that's important, but how well you finish!
> — Jim George

Chapter One: *A Good Start in Life*

Rob saw a white van drive at a snail's pace with the driver looking through the window as if he were searching for something he had lost. Rob's gaze followed the van as it disappeared down the valley. On either side were newly built houses that made the van look like a small toy between two giants.

He saw the same van reach the end of the road. When it turned and moved back, Rob decided to go and meet the driver to find out exactly what he wanted. On seeing him, the van driver stopped and started to chat with him. He was a middle-aged white man with a bushy beard and serious face.

"Hello nice to meet you Sir, you look like you have lost your way. Can I help you?" asked Rob.

"That is exceedingly kind of you. You are the first person to talk to me today. I do not know why people avoid me. Is it because I am an orphan and was adopted by a stranger?" he asked in the lowest, sweetest tone Rob had ever heard. Extending his hand in greeting, the two strangers shook hands.

"My name is Rob, what is your name?" he asked, uncertain if he had asked the right question.

"My name is Jones, and I am a locksmith," he said, opening the back of the van where Rob saw that indeed his van had several tools and locks. The shelves were stacked full of locks and keys of all sizes, most notable a big key cutter at the back of the car.

They started chatting about their lives, about Africa where Rob was born and brought up, about the weather, economics, and politics. Jones told Rob that his mother, unable to raise him, gave him up for adoption when he turned two years. Since that day Jones had never seen nor heard about her.

He also told Rob how he was bullied by other students at school and how he discovered that the world had no place for cowards. With time Jones devised his own ways of protecting himself from bullies by attending martial arts classes. The more they talked, the more they became friends. Jones even made me one key for Rob for free.

On marital life, Jones told Rob that he had never been married and had never been in a committed relationship. The longest he had ever stayed with a woman was six months when he had gone to the pub for a drink. After consuming two pints of beer and chatting with a woman seated on the opposite table, one thing led to another, and they found themselves living together out of convenience rather than love.

"I now live alone. I have no one to talk to in the house, I have no wife or children, and the clock is ticking fast," he reflected. "Whoever said that loneliness and feeling unwanted is the worst poverty was right! Who would hate to enter the house and receive hugs and kisses from the wife? Nobody would hate to share his day's experiences with a member of the other sex," he continued, tears streaming down his face.

"There is someone for everyone. Somewhere a lonely lady is looking to hook up with a man like you. Remember that every dog had its own day," Rob assured him.

As sunset set in, Jones left. If his social life did not change, he would possibly remain single and lonely for the rest of his life. Considering that he had been taken away from his mother's love without his consent, his social life was severely affected. No wonder he had become an introvert in later life.

Time to Reflect:

Every parent has a duty to make sure the children grow up with confidence. They should always feel loved and wanted so that they can love back.

Always listen to your children and ask them to speak their minds. If you tell them something and they ask you why, it is not necessarily arrogance.

If you or your children do not question anything, it means they are fearful. They will develop low self-esteem and start seeing themselves as unworthy in whatever situation they find themselves.

The way they will see themselves is the way other people will see them and that is the way the world will treat them.

Chapter Two: *A Leopard Does Not Change Its Spots*

I could not believe my fortune when I saw a black, sleek convertible BMW car by the roadside advertised for sale. I stopped to take a closer look at the vehicle and was satisfied that was the car that I had always wanted to buy. The price indicated was off my budget, but I felt confident that the seller to give me discount, if I asked him.

Upon reaching home, I called the number where I heard a man's voice.

"Hello, is this Peter who is selling the BMW on Yankee Road?" I asked.

"Yes-Sir, indeed-I-am-the-seller," he replied in the weakest voice that I had ever heard. Shortly after, I heard a long cough.

The more we talked, the more I realised that I was torturing him because of his frequent coughs so I suggested that we meet later in the day when I could examine the car more closely. Meanwhile, I checked online to familiarise myself with all the problems associated with used BMW cars.

We met at the agreed time and was overjoyed that if I played my cards well, the seller would sell it to me at a decent price. I imagined myself driving the car in Central London as I enjoyed the summer sun and felt great!

When the owner arrived, I noticed the man in his early thirties looked painfully thin. He extended his thin hands to greet me as he tried to smile. His skin was dry and worn out.

"Nice to meet you, Peter. I am James," I said.

"Oh, pleasure to meet you too," he replied.

"Just know that you are the luckiest man alive. Sickness is forcing me to sell the car. I am not able to sit on those seats anymore because of my disease," he said in a soft, slow voice.

"Sorry for that, I wish you a quick recovery," I responded gently.

"No, I will not recover. The disease I have is terminal," he replied in a resigned tone. It was sad to hear a man in his thirties say that he was on earth for a limited time.

He entered the car gingerly and showed me around. The interior was sparkling, and the alloy wheels reflected their importance. I then asked him whether he would give me a discount of £1,000 on the purchase price.

"Are you sure you are asking a discount from a dying man? My car is in the best shape!" he concluded.

Finally, we exchanged details and then I paid for the car.

When I returned home and made another thorough check on the car, I was dismayed to discover the vehicle's documents were missing along with the spare tyre. My efforts to call Peter were fruitless since he did not answer.

That night, I used the new car to go to work but when I accelerated the car began making a funny noise as if something was choaking the engine. I also noticed the heating system was faulty; the car remained very cold despite turning on the heating.

When I phoned Peter the following morning, he took forever to answer. I told him that the vehicle had very serious mechanical problems. I requested him to return my money when I returned the car to him.

His unexpected response: "James that is good to hear but I have every reason to believe that when you bought my car, you were of sound mind, and you did not buy it through duress." I affirmed that indeed I was of sound mind, however the car had serious mechanical problems.

"I am not ready to return the money. If you feel that I conned you, take me to court, but just know that by the time the case will be over, I will have died long time!" he concluded. Left with no other alternative, I took the car to the garage for repair.

I could not understand how someone on their deathbed would con another person. Considering Peter's poor health, in his final days on earth, why wouldn't he be decent enough to inform me about the car's faults upfront?

Time to Reflect:

When the deal is too good, think twice, as the saying goes. One should refrain from using emotions instead of facts when engaging in financial transactions. **A leopard does not change its spots**.

Chapter Three: *Guard Your Words*

Max was a lively guy, always cracking jokes that made everyone around him laugh and like him instantly. He was also incredibly generous, always ready to help anyone who needed it. One day, Max told his friends that he'd never celebrated his birthday. They couldn't believe it and encouraged him to throw a party when he turned forty.

Among Max's friends was Timothy, who was looking for some advice from Max about applying for a job at his workplace. Max invited Timothy to his upcoming birthday party so they could chat about it. Since Timothy had never been to Max's place, Max gave him directions.

"Timothy, you're welcome to my birthday! Just head towards town, and when you see the Funeral Home, my house is the next one!" Max said with a grin.

With a puzzled look Timothy replied, "I wish your house was next to a church instead of a funeral home! What made you pick that spot?"

Max, always ready with a joke, laughingly replied; "Don't worry about it. I'm expecting a lot of guests, and if they can't find a place to sleep, I'll just ask the funeral home to let them stay there!"

The party was a blast. Everyone ate, drank, and danced the night away. But just three days later, Max fell ill and passed away. His friends and family arranged to place him in the same funeral home he used to joke about.

Timothy, now heartbroken, took charge of organizing the funds to transport Max's body back to his homeland. While at the funeral home, he noticed an unusually large coffin in one corner. Curious, he asked the funeral director if it was meant for a person or an elephant. The director calmly replied that it was indeed for a person.

Timothy, still in his joking mood, quipped, "Wow, I would've loved to meet this person and ask them why they grew so big! Could you put me in a coffin like that when I pass away?"

The funeral director, playing along, replied, "It's never too late. I promise to take great care of you once you're here."

Timothy jested, "How about this afternoon?"

The director, with a smirk, responded, "Whenever you're ready, we're ready for you!"

As Timothy left the funeral home, he had to cross the road to get to his office. Just as he started crossing, a yellow Volkswagen swerved dangerously towards him, missing him by a whisker. The close call made him remember the joke he'd made about becoming a tenant at the funeral home. Feeling uneasy, he rushed back to the funeral director and apologized, explaining that he was just trying to lighten the mood. The funeral director accepted his apology but gave him a serious reminder: "Nature doesn't joke. What you speak can come true."

Timothy then realized that Max's jokes about the funeral home had become a reality. It made him think deeply about the power of words and how our thoughts and words can shape our lives.

Time to Reflect:

Be careful what you wish for, even in jest.

There are principles in the universe that manifest what we say and think. As a man thinks, so shall he become.

As a man thinketh, so is he.

Chapter Four: *The Answer to Your Problems*

Hurrying down the stairs one morning, I suddenly tripped and hurt my back. Since it didn't really hurt, I brushed it off and rushed out the door, already late for work. I had a busy day ahead, starting with assigning a new task to Laban, one of my junior staff members, before heading to the city, about fifty miles away.

I made it to work and parked in my usual spot without any issues. But as soon as I reached into the back seat to grab my briefcase, a sharp pain shot through my back, just below my shoulder. Thinking it was nothing serious, I pushed through it and walked down the long corridor to my office. The building had around four hundred offices, and after just a few metres, the pain worsened. It felt like my back was being sliced with razor blades!

With every step the pain spread all over my body, especially down my left leg. My toes, thighs, neck, and shoulders were burning. By the time I arrived at my office, I was desperate for the pain to go away, so I decided to stretch out on the sofa. But the pain continued stubbornly like flashes of lightning. Painkillers didn't help.

Then I heard a knock on the door. Fighting through the pain, I managed to open it for Laban.

His eyes were bloodshot, and he looked at me with a grin before bursting out laughing.

"Hey, Boss! You took forever to open the door! I thought you were begging the devil not to send you to the hottest part of hell!" he joked.

My disapproving expression must have shown Laban that I wasn't in the mood for jokes, especially from a junior staff member. But he just laughed again and sat down.

"Look at you! You're walking like you just gave birth! Where's the baby?" he teased.

I couldn't take it anymore. "Laban, enough! If you want to keep your job, stay away from drugs!" I snapped.

Boss, I only drink soda. "Maybe that's what's got me this way," he smirked.

"Just a drink, and you're talking like you're possessed," I shot back. Finally, I explained that my back pain started when I fell down the stairs at home. Laban's continued laughter just fuelled my irritation.

"You probably have a lump on your backbone," he suggested.

I firmly replied, "No, I don't!"

However, Laban wasn't convinced. He insisted that my pain must be from a lump. Without warning, he got up, lifted my shirt, and started feeling around my backbone. To my great surprise, he found a small lump!

"Eureka! This is it! This is what's causing your pain!" he exclaimed, practically jumping with excitement. He then instructed me to lie flat on the floor with my stomach on the carpet. As the pain had become unbearable, I reluctantly agreed.

Laban began massaging the lump and my entire back with surprising skill. After a few minutes, I carefully stood up, stretched, and let out a sigh of relief. The pain was completely gone, thanks to Laban's persistence and quick action.

I couldn't help but wonder, what if Laban hadn't come to the office that day? What if I'd dismissed him because of his silly jokes or because he was just a junior staff member? My original plan was to call an ambulance to take me to the hospital, but thankfully Laban saved me from all that trouble.

Time to Reflect:

Examine your problems with a keen eye and realize that the solution might be closer than you think. Sometimes, the person who can help you is right there, even if you don't always agree with them.

The person who seems insignificant might connect you to someone who holds the key to your health or wealth.

Everyone you meet is a valuable link in the chain of your life. The answer to your problems often lies in the people around you.

Therefore, surround yourself with people of integrity.

Love others and be ready to love some from a distance if needed. Remember, your subconscious mind has an answer to every problem.

> Everyone you meet is a valuable link in the chain of your life. The answer to your problems often lies in the people around you.
> — Lawrence Carlos

Chapter Five: *Breach of Trust*

Betrayal is part of life.

I took a train from my home and headed to London. My first stop was King's Cross St. Pancras, which meant I'd be on the underground, unable to make or take any calls, for the next part of my journey. After disembarking at Elephant and Castle train station, I had a short hundred metre walk to meet my client. Just as I crossed the road leading to Southwark underground station, my phone rang. The mysterious caller had already called ten times. Resisting the urge to ignore it, I figured that whoever had called so persistently must be desperate.

"Hello, James. You've got to help me! I'm in deep trouble. I'm at Heathrow airport, and I'm about to be deported. Please help me," the caller pleaded.

"Who is this?" I asked, trying to place the voice.

"This is John from Edinburgh. I was your neighbour in Willenhall, Birmingham," he explained.

I remembered John from years ago. We'd occasionally meet in a pub and buy each other drinks, though we weren't close friends. "How can I help you, John?" I asked.

"I need a solicitor to stop my deportation order. Like many, I came to England looking for better opportunities," he said.

I valued humanity and felt compelled to help him. "The solicitor I know requires a down payment of £1,800. Can you manage that?" I asked.

John sighed. "I don't have that kind of money right now, and my friends won't be able to raise it immediately. Can you help?"

I called some of his friends, who listened sympathetically but never called back. One neighbour even asked if John would carry clothes for his wife in the village once his deportation order was signed!

"John, a few days ago, you mentioned one of your brothers was terminally ill and required expensive medication. As the breadwinner for your family, your deportation would be a disaster for them," I reminded him.

"I know, James. I'm desperate. Please help," he begged.

"The bank will charge me £30 in interest because my account will be overdrawn. Can you cover that?" I asked.

"James, even if it's a million pounds, I'll pay. Please hurry, otherwise by midnight, the immigration officers will put me on the next flight as a deportee. Please, help a brother," he pleaded.

I took a gamble, called the solicitor, and paid the money. The solicitor took over the case with the immigration department, and John was released.

After his release, John paid me the £1,800 plus the £30 interest charges but never thanked me nor acknowledged my help. Having encountered this kind of attitude many times from friends and relatives, I accepted it.

Two years later, I was having lunch with one of John's relatives in a London restaurant. During our conversation, his relative mentioned, "If I went to Heaven and found you there, I would walk out in protest because you are a bad man."

"Why would you say that?" I asked, shocked.

"Remember what you did to my cousin John? Why did you charge him £30 in interest, pretending it was bank interest?" he asked. I was taken aback that he knew the whole story.

"Yes, you paid £1,800 to his solicitor, but did you have to charge him more? What happened to the values of humanity?" he questioned disapprovingly.

That's when I realized John had told people that I took advantage of him. I felt betrayed but didn't regret helping him. "It was a noble thing to do," I responded.

Time to Reflect:

Beware of people close to you; they are most likely to betray you.

When betrayed, don't lose heart. Understand that in life, some will gain or breach your trust.

Chapter Six: *Old Habits Die Hard*

When I was ten years old, my friend and I decided to visit his home, which meant walking about four miles through a dense forest. The deeper we ventured, the more scared I became, knowing wild animals roamed freely. My friend, however, seemed completely at ease, even humming songs as we walked.

At one point, I asked him if he was scared. "You fear your own shadow! So what if wild animals chase us? We have legs, not blocks of wood!" he replied confidently.

As we approached a hill covered with trees, we saw an old man riding a bicycle at full speed down the hill. He lost control trying to avoid a large trench and fell hard. We ran to help, but by the time we reached him, he was already back on his feet, albeit clearly drunk.

"Oh, John's father, sorry about the accident. Thank God you're not hurt," my friend said, while quickly rifling through the man's coat and trouser pockets. To my shock, he took out some notes and coins and pocketed them. I couldn't believe he would steal from someone in broad daylight.

The old man, in his drunken state, climbed back on his bicycle and cycled away, unaware he had been robbed.

"I'm eighty shillings richer!" my friend boasted.

"No! It's wrong! You've just earned a first-class ticket to hell. You will burn eternally!" I told him.

"To hell with your gods! I am young and rich," he scoffed, trying to give me some of the money. I refused outright.

For the rest of the journey, I couldn't stop wondering how his parents would react when they found out. That evening, during supper, he casually narrated the story of helping the drunk man and taking his money. I wished the ground would swallow me, expecting his parents to punish him severely. To my disbelief, they praised him, seeing him as someone who could survive in the harshest conditions.

Realizing I couldn't stay friends with someone who thought stealing was acceptable, I distanced myself from him, convinced he was on a bad path.

Years later, I learned that after primary school, he became a full-time criminal, spending most of his life in and out of jail. As I write this, he is serving a life sentence. What a waste of life and opportunities! The child who stole money had grown into an adult criminal.

Old habits die hard.

Time to Reflect:

Have you ever had to disconnect from a relationship on moral grounds? Did the person change?

How have your empowering connections and relationships improved your life?

Chapter Seven: Mistaken Identity

One morning, while waiting for the bus to town, I witnessed a horrifying scene. A young boy, aged around fifteen, was being beaten mercilessly by a mob. Some people were kicking and punching him, while others slapped him. Blood was streaming from his mouth, nose, and ears. I crossed the road for a better view, unsure if the boy was dead or alive.

Shortly after, I learned that the boy had broken into a nearby shop to steal food in a desperate bid to stave off his hunger. He had taken a loaf of bread and some milk. The shop owner caught him and raised an alarm, attracting a mob of jobless men at a nearby bus stop. Seeing the boy lying in a pool of blood pained me deeply, especially as a parent.

Some onlookers suggested burning the boy with a tire to teach him and other potential thieves a lesson. Shockingly, the shop owner brought an old tire, doused it in kerosene, and prepared to light it. Horrified, I approached him and pleaded for the boy's life. I even offered to pay for the stolen milk and bread.

After listening to my plea, the shop keeper accused me of being an accomplice in the theft and suggested that I had hired the boy to steal. His loud accusations quickly convinced many in the crowd that I was involved.

I argued that killing the boy was ungodly and would bring curses upon them and their descendants. While most of the mob agreed with me, a smaller group grew increasingly hostile. Realizing the danger, I then produced my company ID to prove my employment with a well-known firm. Unfortunately, few people recognized the company's initials.

Just then, our company van appeared, driven by a colleague. Seeing the van and my colleague vouch for me finally convinced the mob of my innocence. Gratefully, my colleague quickly escorted me away to safety.

Never in my life have I been so scared. Socrates said that no evil shall befall a good man in this world or the next. With a clear conscience, I believe God sent His angels to protect and deliver me that day.

The boy was taken to the hospital, but I never found out if he survived. I often wonder if it was necessary to risk my life for him. *Was my gesture kind or necessary? Was it Godly?*

Whenever I recall that incident, I remember that the boy was simply hungry and desperate.

The curse of poverty forced him to steal. If he had money, he wouldn't have needed to.

Time to Reflect:

Always pray for God to deliver us and our loved ones from the curse of poverty.

Chapter Eight: *A Wise Man Changes His Mind*

On arrival at Heathrow Airport, Priscilla and her two children had come to receive Justus her husband from abroad. Justus' long-time friend James accompanied the family to welcome him to the UK. On this hot summer day, the wife wore a tight Jeans skirt which ended several inches above the knees, accompanied by a sleeveless blouse which exposed a lot of her flesh. When they lived in Africa, Justus had never seen his wife dressed that way; however, since it was his first day in England, he decided to turn a blind eye.

His friend James' hair was well curled and trimmed and he wore a smart moustache. Meanwhile, Justus had let his moustache grow so big he appeared to have two mouths. In Africa, he had an explosive appetite for meat and beer which contributed to his huge tummy. On the way from the airport, one of his children asked him:

"Daddy are you pregnant?" to which he replied, "Yes, I am, why?"

"Your tummy looks so big! You look like you have swallowed a whole cow!" she continued.

"It is a sign of wealth!" he responded proudly.

"I will tell my teacher that my daddy is pregnant!" she announced.

"Dad, tell me, you and Uncle James, who is kinder to mum?" asked the other sibling.

"Why do you ask that, love?" Justus asked in surprise.

"When we went for holiday last summer, Uncle James was so concerned that mum had a cold, and she could not swim. He took her to her room and massaged her poor feet. He is such a good uncle," she stated.

Lost for words, Justus let his children tell him more. When he enquired where the children were when their mum's feet were being massaged, they informed him that they were praying in the sitting room.

"Uncle wanted to show mum that he cared. But mum was just crying as her feet were being massaged. Mum was very mean!" she concluded.

Priscilla, overhearing the conversation, quickly interjected: "Yes, we went for the summer holidays with James and his family, and we had an enjoyable time!"

Unsure how to react, Justus decided not to draw a serious conclusion from what his child had just revealed. It was too early to judge. Meanwhile James was busy driving the car, ignoring the ongoing conversation.

Justus was overjoyed to be in a magnificent country where everything looked well planned.

On the way, his children were all over him since they had not been together for five years. While he was in deep conversation with his children, his wife and James were busy chatting away. He was amazed to hear Priscilla laughing uncontrollably in response to whatever James said.

Back in Africa, Justus was not used to seeing his wife talk to another man so freely in his presence; he wondered whether Priscilla was the same wife who left him to relocate to England five years earlier.

After an hour and a half, they arrived at Priscilla's house. As she alighted, through her short skirt and blouse Justus was shocked to see her navel but pretended not to notice.

There was extraordinarily little conversation between Justus and his wife despite not having seen each other face to face in a long while. By contrast, both James and Priscilla had so much to talk about, especially matters relating to work and world politics.

In the house, Priscilla prepared breakfast which they all ate heartily as they caught up with their past lives. Before leaving them to head back to his own family, James promised to return later in the afternoon so that he could show Justus around.

At exactly 2 pm James arrived. He took Justus for a drink as a sign of friendship and to explain what to expect from abroad and what abroad expected from him.

"Now that you have stepped onto British soil, you will have to leave your ego in the plane otherwise you will never get ahead in life," James began in a serious tone.

"Meaning what...?" asked Justus, intrigued.

"While in this country, it is not for you to choose the job, the job will choose you," James elaborated.

"What is the worst job I should expect?" Justus asked, lighting a cigarette and exhaling a cloud of smoke.

"Once you have proper documents, apply for jobs with employment agencies. If you get even a mortuary job cleaning corpses, just do it. In the end you will be paid in British pounds which is a strong currency," James replied.

"What else?" Justus asked, fixing his eyes on James as if he was a government hangman.

"At times you can expect jobs in care homes where you take care of the elderly, you clean and feed them with care. Alternatively, you can work as a security guard or take up factory work," he stated.

"I have no problem with any other job, but cleaning the elderly? You mean I get to clean someone who is the age of my grandmother? Are you serious that these are the jobs you people do here? I wish I knew," Justus exclaimed with deep regret that he had resigned from his highly respected professional job in Africa.

James continued, "If you used to order your wife and children around, this has got to stop! You are now in a country where the rule of law applies."

Justus remembered that when James left that morning, he had quarrelled with his wife because of the way she was dressed. He was particularly critical of how much flesh she was displaying to the entire world. His wife told him that he should have realised that he was no longer in his home country but in a country where women are conscious of the fashion trends.

"What?! Who is the leader of the house then if I cannot talk in my own house?!" he asked in disbelief.

"I mean exactly that, Justus. Your machismo will not work here. Your wife has the power to chase you out of your house and the police will forbid you from being around her within a certain radius. She can even have a boyfriend the same day you leave if she so wishes," James continued, for good measure.

"Why am I a man then?" he asked defensively.

"You must change your ways otherwise you will eventually not only risk losing your family but also being on the wrong side of the law. In this country, if you stress your wife and she informs the police, you will be in for it," James warned.

"Furthermore, you will be arrested and charged with causing grievous bodily harm. If you end up with a criminal record, that is where your hard life abroad will start."

"You will struggle to get a decent job, and your insurance premiums will be extremely high. Besides, you will find it hard to get credit facilities from financial institutions. When in Western countries, train yourself to have eyes and not see and have ears and do not hear as far as some issues are concerned," James wisely admonished him.

After five years, James and Justus had not met, since Justus always thought that James had messed with his wife while he was away. Regrettably, Justus disregarded James' sage advice and continued to physically and emotionally abuse his wife and children.

To safeguard their children's safety alongside her own, Priscilla reported him to the police numerous times. The social welfare department eventually advised the couple to separate for the sake of peace.

After they separated Justus lost the joy of seeing his young children growing up. Rather than find work, Justus chose to rely on the social benefit from the Department of Pensions. When asked why he never worked, he would say that after talking with James, it became apparent to him that the only jobs available in the West would lower his dignity.

Moreover, he could not imagine himself working in a care home, security firm or factory after having worked as a professional in his home country.

Justus lost his family because he failed to adjust to the new system in his adopted country. To top it all, due to his stinking attitude and criminal record attached to his name, he could not get a job or credit facilities so his life in the West became very hard.

Time to Reflect:

What words of advice would your share with someone struggling to adjust to their new surroundings and culture?

Remember:

A wise man changes his mind, a fool never.

> A wise man changes his mind,
> a fool never.
> — Lawrence Carlos

Chapter Nine: *Birds of a Feather Flock Together*

My friendship with Tom began back in Form One. In the dormitory, our beds were right next to each other, which naturally brought us closer. We both came from similar backgrounds—straight out of the village. In the village, people didn't perceive themselves as poor; it was just life as we knew it.

Before I joined Form One, one of my elder brothers gave me some advice: if I wanted to get the best out of high school, I had to love the school. He also suggested that I become friends with the smartest boy in class. His reasoning was simple: if my best friend was academically sharp, I could learn from him and improve my own grades.

It didn't take long to realize that Tom was incredibly bright. So, I made sure we became the best of friends. We studied and ate lunch together, and even wrote letters together to girls from nearby schools. One of his girlfriends even called him *Tom and Jerry*, a nickname I also used, which he didn't mind at all.

Throughout our school life, we enjoyed each other's company so much that each holiday we'd visit each other's homes in turns. We trusted each other completely. Tom would often open and read my letters before I did. If it was from a girl he didn't like, he'd suggest tearing it up, and I'd have to beg him to let me read it first.

I'd do the same with his letters, playfully refusing to reveal what his girlfriend had written.

"Tom and Jerry, you won't believe what Susan wrote to you. She's dumping you after dreaming about a devil that looked like a young man. Brace yourself for the shock!" I'd tease him, prompting him to lose his appetite until I finally let him read the letter.

After completing our 'O' levels we prepared to join 'A' levels but ended up at different schools. Still, our friendship remained strong. Tom would often stop by my place on his way home and spend a week with us. We genuinely wanted the best for each other.

After two years, we went to different higher learning institutions, and when we both got jobs, we decided to rent a two-bedroom house together, situated in an average neighbourhood in the city. Financially, it made sense. However, six months later the company Tom worked for unexpectedly went under and he lost his job. As his best friend, I didn't mind supporting him with the little I was earning. After all, a friend in need is a friend indeed.

Eventually, Tom landed an excellent job in the city. It came with a hefty salary, fringe benefits including two holiday trips to any destination in the world, and a generous house and car allowance.

His one-week entertainment allowance was equivalent to my monthly salary. Due to the nature of his job, management insisted he move to a neighbourhood that matched his new social status, which prompted Tom to move out of our shared place.

Initially, we met every Friday for coffee, but as time passed, Tom became 'too busy' for me. The regular calls also dwindled. Before, we'd chat on the phone even when there was nothing urgent, but after a while, months would go by without a word from him. It was clear that Tom's social status had risen to a level far above mine.

One day, I was in my office when the phone rang in my boss's office. Since my boss was out for lunch, I answered the line. Surprised to hear Tom's voice after such a long time, I began, excited to catch up: "Hello, Tom! You've been so quiet lately!"

"I'm fine. Is Jacob around?" he asked quietly.

"C'mon, how can you ask about Mr Jacob when I'm the one talking to you? Should I start calling you Mr Tom and Jerry?" I joked.

There was total silence on the other end, and I thought Tom had hung up.

"Hello, Tom? Are you still there?" I asked, puzzled by his distant behaviour.

"YES! I'm here. I was waiting for you to finish your nonsense!" he snapped harshly. I couldn't believe my ears.

"Am I talking to Tom?" I enquired again, still in shock.

"Yes! I know it's you. If I wanted to call you, I would have. Next time, do me a favour—don't ever say such nonsense to me again!" he barked before hanging up.

In stunned silence I replaced the receiver and returned to my office. Was this the same Tom I had supported just a year ago? The same school friend?

While I tried to make sense of it all, an inner voice whispered that I was no longer a bird of the same feather with him; I'd do well to accept that.

Meanwhile, Tom's success had skyrocketed. He appeared in the media, gave press conferences and become a national sensation. As his ladder of success climbed higher, he started buying property in upscale neighbourhoods; his tenants were ambassadors and corporate directors of global companies. I couldn't help but wonder what magic he had worked to achieve such success.

When we unexpectedly bumped into each other at a petrol station one day, Tom apologized for what he had said during that phone call. I told him I felt deeply betrayed by a friend I had trusted, and continued, "Trust is like virginity—it's only broken once."

He also mentioned that he hadn't married yet because he hadn't found 'Miss Right.' I wanted to tell him that his arrogance and pride were the likely reasons why. After all, no self-respecting woman would want to be with someone who didn't care about what came out of his mouth.

Unsurprisingly, Tom was no longer in my circle of friends, not because of his success, but because of his arrogance. He might have reached a higher social class, but that didn't give him the right to act inhumanly towards me or others. I wasn't badly off, but in his eyes, I wasn't a bird of his feather anymore.

I remember my pastor once said that the easiest way to lose your wife is when her boss is a highly intelligent man.

At home, she'll compare you to him and realize that when she asked God for a husband, she was expecting something more.

The same goes for friends—if your friends are extremely intelligent and you don't tap into their knowledge, you risk losing your wife to them because they and your wife are birds of a feather.

Time to Reflect:

If you don't add value to yourself, your life will remain stagnant, and you won't see any transformation throughout the year.

The solution? Add value to yourself so you can attract people who challenge and uplift you to another level. That way, you'll become a bird of a feather with those who can help you grow.

Birds of a feather flock together.

Add value to yourself so you can attract people who challenge and uplift you to another level. That way, you'll become a bird of a feather with those who can help you grow.
- Lawrence Carlos

Chapter Ten: *One Man's Meat*

One Man's Meat is Another Man's Poison

In primary school, we couldn't wait to join high school. We were told that high school offered freedom, if it didn't compromise our morals. Our teachers also informed us that high school students enjoyed a varied diet, unlike the maize and beans staple in our village. This promise of a better life motivated us to work hard.

My role model was a young man named Solomon, who had completed primary school four years ahead of me. He had excelled academically and was highly respected in the village. Known for his eloquence and ability to mediate disputes, he earned the nickname 'King Solomon'. Naturally, I admired him and hoped to follow in his footsteps.

When I got admitted to Solomon's former school, I was overjoyed. I believed that if the school produced students like Solomon, it must be exceptional. He assured me there was no bullying at his school. So, I confidently waited in the school's administration office. When other students asked where I was from, I proudly told them I was from the same village as Solomon.

Around 2:00 pm, we were taken to the dormitories. While everyone else was nervous, I felt calm because I knew Solomon, the village genius.

Soon, older students joined us and began asking strange, personal questions—typical bullying behaviour. Naively, I couldn't wait to mention my connection to Solomon.

"I come from Nyas village," I said proudly.

"Oh! Then you must know Solomon!" they responded.

"Of course! He's my first cousin," I lied, hoping to impress them. In the stunned silence that followed, I thought they were admiring me. Shortly after, someone asked how many plates of food I needed to feel full. I replied that one plate was enough, just like anyone else.

"Really? What about Solomon, your cousin?" they asked.

"Just one plate, of course!" I answered.

"If you found us smoking, would you tell the Head Teacher?" they asked in unison.

"No, definitely not!" I replied.

"Would you feel guilty if a student got expelled for smoking because of you?" they continued.

"Not at all!" I answered confidently.

Suddenly, the atmosphere changed. One boy grabbed me by the neck and demanded I apologize on Solomon's behalf.

"Do you know I was suspended because of your cousin? He thought he was a god just because he was the Head Boy," he said, veins bulging.

As he shook my neck, another boy claimed Solomon had repeatedly punished him, and now wanted revenge.

"I swear by my grandmother, you must pay for your cousin's sins," he said, pricking his thumb with a needle and drinking the blood to show his seriousness.

"It's not in vain that I've spilled this blood. You will pay by blood for your cousin's actions," he declared.

The crowd erupted, with students whistling, cursing, and calling for my blood. I felt like I was at hell's gates. Fortunately, the Head Boy noticed the commotion and intervened. The students scattered as he approached. After listening to my story, he advised me to deny knowing Solomon if asked again, then transferred me to another dormitory where I found peace.

In our identical new uniforms, it was hard to tell one first-year student from another, a blessing which helped me blended in. To me, Solomon was a hero, but to others, he was a tyrant.

I learned a valuable lesson that day: Never be quick to declare your association with someone without first understanding how others perceive them.

Time to Reflect:

When in unfamiliar territory, take your time before mentioning your connections. You never know how the person you admire is viewed by others.

Speaking highly of someone could unintentionally align you with their enemies.

Remember: *One man's meat is another person's poison.*

Chapter Eleven: *One Day at A Time*

Our Headteacher instructed us to assemble in the main college hall ready for the special guest who was to give us a talk. We were all seated at exactly 5:00 pm, eagerly waiting. Within a few minutes, the Headteacher entered with a tall, dark, middle-aged man. He had a well-trimmed moustache and captivating smile. As soon as he entered, all the ladies screamed and clapped for him.

The Headteacher introduced him as 'Doctor Tom', who started his schooling in N province and went to the most prestigious high school in Kenya for 'O' and 'A' levels. After completing high school, he went to America for further studies, thanks to the famous 'Airlift' program by a well-known politician from the N region.

"I could talk all day about our guest, but let him take over from me now," concluded the Headteacher.

As Tom stood up from his seat and smiled at us, we noticed that he had difficulty standing. His walking was slow and unsteady. He waved briefly and then began addressing us.

"Mmmmm... mm... m... my nnnn... name... is... doc... doc... Dr. Tooooo... Tom! I was.... t. t.... t... teaching in the Univer... sssity... University of Michigan...." he slurred. His speech was characterized by stammering and incoherence.

He told us that he had been a student at the University of Michigan, then at Harvard University, and eventually returned to Michigan as a lecturer. He had taught at many universities in America, Europe, and Australia and was grateful for his academic accomplishments. His plan was to return to Kenya and build a university for the poor and bright students.

In 1969, he came to Kenya to visit his friends and relatives in the region where he was born and raised. On the day he landed in the country, a popular politician was gunned down in the capital city, 500 kilometres away. Many believed the murder was politically motivated by those in power. The news spread like wildfire, leading to violent countrywide demonstrations.

Despite being from a different tribe, Tom was a local celebrity due to his academic credentials. Unaware of the current local tensions, he had ended up in the murdered politician's town that day. The locals, angered by the politician's death, identified him and beat him mercilessly. The worst memory he had was being hit on the back of the head with a club until he passed out.

After lying unconscious in hospital for many months, Tom finally woke up. However, the serious injuries affected his speech, and he began to stammer. Sadly, his career crumbled in one day because he could no longer return to America to teach. His big dream of building a university for poor students never materialized because of his health.

Despite his difficulties, Tom requested our help to finance the publication of a book about his life because he believed he still had much to offer through his writings.

Time to Reflect:

Good and terrible things happen to everyone living. When good breaks come our way, we should grab them and never let them slip away.

Since no situation is permanent, we should make the most of the good times.

When we wake up healthy and strong, we should thank God.

Let us endeavour to live each day as if it were our last on earth because that will be our reality one day.

Chapter Twelve: *From Setback to Success*

A Problem is A Lesson

After the bomb blast in the city, it never occurred to us that our industry would be most affected. Our main business came from America and Western Europe, but after the attack, business dwindled, and many staff members were made redundant.

As the person responsible for preparing the final dues, I faced the heart-wrenching task of meeting with those who had lost their jobs. Words cannot describe how sad it was to see colleagues in tears, fretting about their future. One colleague, whose wife had just given birth, confided that this was the worst possible time to lose his job. I tried to console him, saying that when one door closes, another one opens.

Unknown to me, my name was also on the redundancy list. Shortly after preparing everyone else's final dues, I received a letter informing me that I was to leave my job the following day. Gripped by shock, I looked up at the ceiling, hoping for answers, but found none. As if to bring the point home, I returned from lunch to find a new lock on my office door, denying me access.

Then my boss called me in, asking me to train my replacement. Despite my confusion and disbelief, I did my best, hoping a new opportunity would soon arise.

What was I going to do without my income? How would I pay my bills? I was accustomed to driving a nice car and eating at good restaurants. How could I support my wife and small children? Staring at the letter, I wondered if this was a cruel joke. I had always encouraged others who lost their jobs, without realising I would soon be in their shoes.

The next day, I left my job, bitter and frustrated. My four-year-old son kept asking where I worked, and I lied, saying I was a cook for Michael Jackson, his hero. He saw me as a hero and told all the neighbourhood children.

Since I had to put food on the table, I began to think outside the box for new ways to make money. I registered a company and started supplying items to individuals and organizations. Some clients paid promptly, while others delayed, teaching me valuable business lessons.

By God's grace, the business picked up. At one point, I made profits equivalent to two years of my previous salary from a single supply! This experience taught me the importance of having a side business as a safety net. One should not be too comfortable with a day job, as opportunities are always waiting to be discovered.

Looking back, redundancy was the best thing that happened to reveal my business acumen and other talents.

It also opened the door to travel the world, something I treasure deeply.

Time to Reflect:

Good and bad things happen to everyone. When good breaks come, grab them and never let them slip away.

No situation is permanent. Live each day to the fullest, as if it were your last, because one day it will be.

Problems are not always from the devil; sometimes, they are God's way of shaking our comfort zones to elevate us to another level.

If a relationship or business is failing, it might be a sign to move on and explore other opportunities. God will guide you if you ask Him.

There are no problems, only feedback and lessons.

The challenges you face are opportunities in disguise.

Chapter Thirteen: *Look Beyond Behaviours*

When I first arrived in the West, my first job was what you might call a 'dirty' job. My boss had called my host to see if I'd be interested in filling in for a sick worker, and since I needed the money, I agreed.

"Thanks for helping out, he said. Take a train from your place, head to Kings Cross, then catch the underground to Paddington. From there, take the train to Slough." He spoke with an accent I could barely understand. Moreover, I had no idea where these places were. It sounded like he was speaking in tongues. As a recent arrival to England, with no experience of travelling locally by train, I was completely lost.

Fifteen minutes later, my phone rang again. It was my new boss, clearly agitated. "Are you serious? You're still at home? Didn't you say you were going to Slough?" he barked.

"Boss, I didn't catch what you said. All I heard was 'Sly,'" I replied, trying to keep my cool.

"What are you talking about?" he snapped.

"Well, I don't know my way to the train station," I tried to explain, but he rudely cut me off.

"If you can't talk to me with respect, you can keep your job!" I shot back, frustrated.

"This is a new contract, and I can't afford to lose it. I have an hour to get someone to work, or it will go to my competitors," he retorted.

As I prepared to head to the station, suddenly the cold weather outside hit me. Coming from Africa, where temperatures sometimes reached 37°C, the freezing -5°C weather was a shock to my system. After quickly donning on some warm clothes, I called a cab and headed out. My host had helpfully mentioned that his friend would meet me at the station with a mobile phone for communication.

On the train to London, I marvelled at the English countryside, but at Kings Cross I was overwhelmed by the underground system's complexity. I asked the railway staff for directions, but most of what they said went over my head. Finally, I reached Paddington and called my boss, hoping for some guidance and maybe a bit of praise for getting this far.

"Boss, I'm finally at Paddington! That was a rough ride, but I made it!" I announced confidently.

"Didn't I tell you to go to Slough? What is wrong with you?" he shouted.

"You mean my journey isn't over yet?" I asked, completely deflated.

"My goodness, what planet are you from?" he muttered.

"From Mars, and you're from Venus!" I shot back angrily.

"Don't give me that nonsense. I'm about to lose this contract, and you're playing games!" he yelled.

"Did you just call me an idiot?" I asked, shocked.

"Yes! Who do you think you are?" he screamed.

We exchanged harsh words, then he hung up on me. There I was, in a strange city, my chance to earn some money quickly slipping away. My family back home needed funds for upkeep, meanwhile I was stranded with just £5.36 in my pocket—barely enough to get by.

I thought about using the money to start my journey back home, but with no friends or family in London, along with the harsh winter cold, I wasn't sure how I'd survive. The cold air felt like being trapped in a freezer.

Desperate, I decided to approach a man of colour at the station. "Hi Sir, my name is James, and I'm lost in this city…," I began, visibly shivering from the cold.

The man, adjusting his dreadlocks, looked at me and said, "Respect, man! Why are you reporting to me? I'm not your mummy!"

His response left me wondering if everyone in London spoke like this or if the gods in Africa were punishing me.

Just then, my phone rang. It was John, my boss's friend, who had given me the mobile phone. Relieved to hear his voice, I shared my predicament.

"I'm in Paddington, and I don't have enough fare! Please help me, I'm desperate!" I pleaded.

"I'm not here to solve your problems. First tell me, why did you insult Mr Lee?" he asked angrily.

"He insulted me first, so I told him what I thought of him," I explained.

"Did you really tell him he should be a pathologist because he's inhuman?" John's voice sounded incredulous.

"Yes, because he doesn't know how to deal with living humans!" I replied.

John, disappointed, informed me that if I didn't change my attitude, life in London would be unmanageable. His words began to make sense—I was already suffering.

"Please, John, help me!" I begged in desperation.

My anguished tone touched John's heart, prompting him to ask after a few moments of silence, "Are you sorry for insulting Mr Lee?"

"Yes, of course!" I said, even though I would have agreed to anything at that point just to get out of the freezing cold.

"That ticket will take you to Camden Town. When you get off, cross the road and follow the first exit to the right. Walk down Prince of Wales Road for a mile, and you'll find a construction site called 'D & L Development Ltd.' Ask for Joseph," he instructed.

Although I could barely process the information, somehow I managed to follow his directions. After a cold and hungry thirty-minute walk, I arrived at the site where a young man wearing a reflective jacket and hard hat greeted me.

"Hello, I was sent by John," I said.

"I know," he replied, looking me up and down as if I were a fossil that refused to become extinct.

"How can I help you? You're just standing there saying nothing! **Talk**!" he demanded.

I was stunned by how this young man, who looked ten years younger than me, could shout at me like that.

Eventually, Joseph led me into the warm, inviting canteen, where I finally started to feel human again. After a while, he even made us tea and offered me bread, which I gratefully devoured.

As we chatted, Joseph gave me some tough advice. "If you want to get the best out of anything, you've got to show some love toward it. You came here from a developing country and instead of giving yourself time to love this place, you're already hating it? If you don't change your attitude, it will be a freezing day in hell before you make it in London."

Curious, I asked Joseph more about his life and Europe in general, but he cut me off.

"The problem with you is that once you start talking, you don't close your mouth!" he said.

Feeling the need to ease the tension, I apologized for asking too many questions. He then asked if I was ready for induction, which is when I realized that John had sent me here to work as a security officer, not to get fare home. I was shocked when Joseph told me I'd be paid more than I had ever earned in a single day.

Joseph took down my details when we returned to the canteen. He also asked if I'd be interested in working at their site in Slough.

"Funny enough, Slough is where I was supposed to work tonight, but the boss was very rude," I said.

Joseph, or rather Mr Lee as I later found out, turned out to be a man of his word. He left the site at 9:00 pm, but not before buying me Chinese food from a nearby restaurant. That meal felt like a taste of heaven. Later that night, I received a call from John, who casually informed me that the next morning Mr Lee would come to take me home.

"Did you say 'Mr Lee'?" I asked, shocked.

"Yes, and incidentally, Joseph is Mr Lee. He's the same person," John concluded.

I was floored. The whole time I had been talking to the boss himself! The next morning, Mr Lee arrived in a sleek BMW, acting as though nothing had happened. As we drove, I finally apologized for our argument.

"What disagreement? he asked, brushing it off. That's in the past. Today is a new day."

As we cruised down the motorway, he explained that his frustration the previous night was due to the risk of losing a £100,000-a-month contract. That was when I began to see things from his perspective.

"Always look beyond behaviour and stop the prejudice. If you don't, you'll lose a lot in relationships, business, or otherwise," he advised.

Fast forward eight years later, I found myself in a similar situation, running my own business in London. One of my guards was late, and my furious client was threatening to cancel our contract.

As I screamed at the guard over the phone, I suddenly realized I was behaving just like Mr Lee had all those years ago.

Mr Lee became a role model for me in England. He taught me to rise above mediocrity and see beyond people's behaviour. More importantly, his attitude toward life made him successful.

Time to Reflect:

Consider areas where you need to make a shift to rise higher in life.

Where do you need to transform your mind and attitude in your relationships, business, career?

Remember, *your attitude determines your altitude.*

> Your attitude determines your altitude.
> — Zig Ziglar

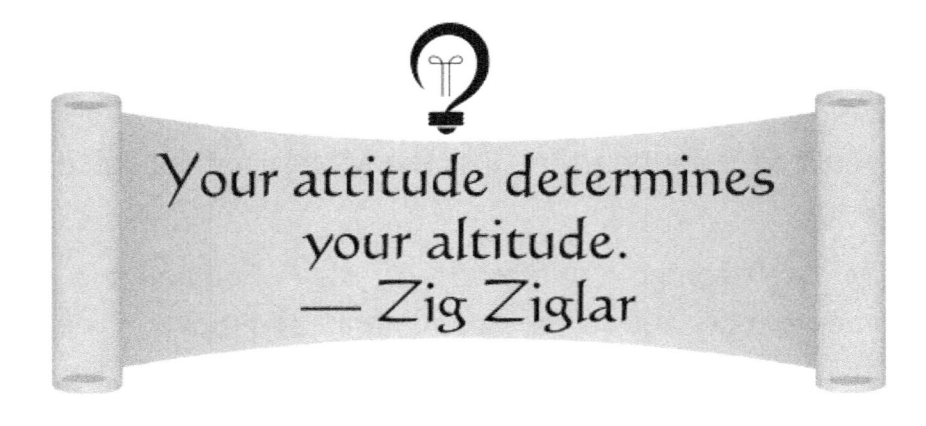

Chapter Fourteen: *Denied By Character*

Jamie and Lena were high school classmates, but they came from different worlds—Jamie from Central Province and Lena from the Coast. Lena's background was a mix; her father, a European, had returned to Europe after separating from her mother, leaving Lena and her mother behind. Lena stood out not just because of her tall, slender frame and long, curly black hair, but also because of her melodious voice.

While most students spent hours poring over books, Lena seemed to glide through her studies with ease, never understanding how others could study for more than three hours. Yet, when exam results came in, Lena was always at the top with straight A's. Outside of academics, she was equally involved in extracurricular activities, excelling in athletics and ball games.

Many boys dreamed of dating Lena, but she made it clear she was only interested in friendship. Her primary focus was on achieving the highest academic marks in the country, and she was confident she had already aced the final exams. Lena's sharp mind and eloquence in school debates earned her respect among her peers and admiration for her command of the English language.

One Saturday afternoon, after the final exams were over, Jamie found himself alone with Lena in their classroom.

It was the first time they'd had a real conversation, despite sharing the same class for two years.

"You're an incredible student, Lena. I'm really going to miss you after we finish school," Jamie admitted.

"Are you serious? You'll miss me?" Lena asked with a smile.

"Absolutely! I've never met anyone so talented in both sports and academics. You're one of a kind," Jamie said, clearly in awe.

"Thanks, Jamie. I think it's all in the genes—my father always told me to believe in myself, to see myself as a champion before anything else," she explained.

"Considering how brilliant you are, do you ever find yourself questioning if it's real, being so good at everything?" Jamie asked, curiously.

"We live in a world full of possibilities. Any knowledge we want is within reach. Scientists say we only use ten percent of our brains—imagine what we could do if we used a hundred percent!" Lena replied with a twinkle in her eye.

As they talked, two boys joined them, prompting Lena to excuse herself. But before she left, she invited Jamie to take a walk with her since it was their last day at school.

As they strolled outside, Lena confessed that she found Jamie easy to talk to and thought he was interesting.

"Lena, how are you planning to get back to the Coast? Are you flying, taking a train, or catching a bus?" Jamie inquired.

"I think I'll hitch a ride. I have bus fare, but I usually get offered lifts by men," she said nonchalantly.

Jamie was taken aback. "You're full of surprises, Lena. You mean you'll hitch a ride all the way to the Coast from here?"

"Yes! I'm not afraid of anyone. My dad taught me to believe in myself and never let fear control me," she responded confidently.

"But what if the person who offers you a lift is dangerous, like a rapist? Isn't that too risky?" Jamie pressed, genuinely concerned for her safety.

Lena smiled. "I know I have stunning looks, but if things get rough, I'm a Black Belt in Taekwondo. I can handle myself."

"If I were your dad, I'd tell you to use public transport to stay safe. Please consider it, Lena—we'd hate to see anything happen to you," Jamie pleaded.

"Getting lifts has never been a problem for me. You know I'm a person of integrity, even if you've only known me for a short time," she reassured him.

"Do these men ask you out after they drop you off?" Jamie asked, intrigued.

"All the time! But I just tell them I'm born again and believe in sex after marriage. That usually puts them off," Lena laughed.

They talked until sunset, and before parting ways, Jamie invited Lena to visit him in his village. She was delighted by the invitation and promised to visit and write to him. As they said their goodbyes, Jamie felt like the luckiest guy on earth.

A few weeks later, on a Wednesday evening, Jamie was listening to the radio when an unexpected announcement jolted him to the core:

*...**We regret to announce the death of Lena... the cortege will leave... funeral home and the burial will be held at... cemetery**...*

Jamie couldn't believe it—Lena, dead? How could it be? He hadn't been able to eat or sleep that night, replaying their last conversation in his mind. When he went to pick up his exam results, he asked his classmates if they had heard about Lena's death. Most hadn't, but one teacher confirmed the tragic news.

Apparently, Lena had accepted a lift from a stranger who, unbeknownst to her, was on a suicide mission. He drove the car off a cliff, and both died instantly.

The news of her death sent shockwaves through everyone who knew her. How could someone so smart and full of promise meet such a tragic end?

It wasn't her intellect that failed her, but her inability to recognize that wisdom is more than just knowledge—it's the ability to apply that knowledge in a way that protects and sustains us.

Lena was every teacher's dream student—brilliant, driven, and full of potential. She could grasp complex concepts with ease and her creativity was unmatched. But despite all her gifts, Lena had a weakness—a tendency to make impulsive decisions without fully considering the consequences.

On that fateful day, Lena made a choice that seemed trivial but was rooted in carelessness and a lack of discernment. She ignored the signs, believing she was too smart to fall into any danger. But intelligence alone couldn't save her from the consequences of her actions.

Lena's story soberly reminds us of the limits of intelligence. No matter how bright or talented we are, we're all vulnerable to the consequences of our choices. Destructive habits, when left unchecked, can lead even the most brilliant minds to ruin. Lena's life, so full of promise, ended not because she wasn't smart enough, but because she didn't realize that true wisdom lies in understanding our own weaknesses and taking steps to overcome them.

Her death was a loss not only of a bright young woman but of all the potential she carried. It's a sobering thought that talent and intelligence, without the guidance of discernment and care, can lead to a tragic and premature end.

Lena's story outlines the importance of self-awareness and the need to transform our mindset before it's too late.

Time to Reflect:

Have you identified any destructive habits in someone close to you that need to be addressed to avoid self-destruction?

What words of advice and caution can you share to support their renewed mindset?

The graveyard is the richest place on earth, because it is here that you will find all the hopes and dreams that were never fulfilled. The books that were never written, the songs that were never sung, the inventions that were never shared, the cures that were never discovered.
- Dr Myles Munroe

Chapter Fifteen: *Your Skeleton will Come to Life*

Be mindful of your actions.

Some years back in England, we were celebrating my son's birthday where I had thrown a relatively big party. My friends from all over the UK had attended accompanied by their friends.

After the party, those unable to return to their respective homes ended up spending the night at my place. Beer and meat flowed in plenty, adding to the culinary delight. After everyone had indulged in food and drink, the guests, young and old, took to the disco floor to show off their rhythmic dance prowess.

As the night progressed, I noticed one friend's guest's unruly behaviour. His dance moves were characterised by embarrassing obscene gestures, As the host, I was also embarrassed by this character's raised voice and disgustingly distasteful words to traditional vernacular songs. Escorting him outside, I kindly requested him to mind his tongue because he was making everybody uncomfortable.

"So what if I am making people uncomfortable! I don't sleep in anybody's tummy! All those complaining about me can all take a hike to hell!" he retorted carelessly.

"If you continue to breach the peace, I will call the police, and you will be arrested. You'd better shut your mouth from now on!" I warned him exasperatedly.

"Wow! You could have called the police yesterday! I will tell them that you were not born but hatched!" he retorted, laughing stupidly.

The more he talked the more he irritated me. At some point I considered reporting him to the police. When we returned to the house, I was pleasantly surprised to witness his behaviour change from unruly to quiet and composed. Afterwards, he became sleepy and started snoring. My friend (who was his friend) and I took him to a nearby B&B to sleep off the hangover until the following day.

The following morning, I bid my guests goodbye as they headed to work. Before my friend left to get his 'drunken, rude and disorderly' friend from the B&B hotel, I politely suggested that in future he should only visit my place with people of integrity not timewasters.

Many years later, as I drove to the North of England several hundred miles from home, my car suddenly broke down. The bitter winter cold and snow hit me like a ton of bricks. Parked by the roadside, it dawned on me that since I had forgotten to renew my breakdown cover, no car rescue company would come to help me.

I called my best friend to request if I could possibly use his cover, but he did not answer the phone. Meanwhile, my phone's charge was running low. If I did not come up with a quick solution, the freezing winter cold would bite me to death. With every passing minute I hoped my friend would call me back.

By God's grace, he finally called me, and I explained my challenge and where I was.

"Ah! You are just outside Lamar's place. I will ask him to give you any support you need," he said.

"Who is Lamar?" I asked jokingly, my teeth gnashing as if I was on death row.

After about fifteen minutes, Lamar arrived, overjoyed to see me.

"So it's you! Welcome to the North, only mountains don't meet! I have always wanted to see you! God is great!" he said as he called his rescue service. At first, I had not recognised him but after examining him more closely, I remembered he was the once unruly man I had almost called cops for years ago in my house!

When he suggested we go to his house, I almost jumped out of my skin just in case he remembered what I had told him on that fateful day.

When we reached his house, he introduced me to his wife and two lovely children.

There was a shiny new Mercedes Benz parked outside which he informed me belonged to his wife and children. He then reminded me how I had thrown a big party for them and how they all enjoyed it.

Recalling his unsightly behaviour, he informed me that he was going through a lot because his relationship with his previous girlfriend had just hit the rocks. Devastated by the whole ordeal he had resulted to drunkenness to escape the pain. He then apologised profusely for his bad behaviour.

"Lamar, on my part, I forgive you seventy times seven times!" I told him unreservedly.

As I slept in one of his comfortable guest rooms, I kept wondering what might have happened had I called the cops to arrest him that day. With all he was going through, how much more damage would a prison sentence have affected his life and destiny? Just how embarrassing would I have felt if I had thrown him out of my house that day, only to ask him for help years later?

Time to Reflect:

At some point in our lives, we all make mistakes. We should always give people a second chance. Until one has experienced what someone has gone through, he should not be very quick to judge them.

Before you take any action against anybody, think about the repercussion it will have on them.

We are our brother's keeper; let us treat each other with dignity and respect.

What you do today, good or bad is a 'skeleton' that will come to life one day soon. Be warned.

Chapter Sixteen: *Do Not Betray Anybody*

I had gone to register for professional exams like many others pursuing a similar career path. Arriving thirty minutes late, I was disappointed to find a long queue. Annoyingly, the staff were taking an exceptionally long time to check each applicant's certificates.

In front of me in the queue was a medium-height, light-skinned, smart, elegant lady. Next to her was a short, stout man engrossed in reading a newspaper. From their laughter and interaction, it was clear they knew each other well.

To pass the time, I started reading my own newspaper. As I was going through the first page, I overheard the lady speaking to the man beside her.

"Leonardo, would you mind offering me a lift to town? I need to visit my dad who lives in the eastern part of the city," she requested.

"It's alright, Joan, so long as you don't bring too much luggage. You're welcome," he replied in his deep, booming voice.

Hearing his voice, I suddenly remembered a unique voice from my last year in high school. I had a friend and classmate named Leon, a short, plump guy with a round head, known for his highly intelligent arguments.

We had shared a class and dormitory, interacting a lot. He had joined our school to repeat his exams, driven by an insatiable thirst to join university.

Curious, I raised my head to catch a glimpse of him, but he avoided eye contact. When our eyes finally met, he didn't seem to recognize me. I decided to ask him directly.

"Hi, you look like someone I know. Are you Leon?" I asked.

"Well, well... it depends," he replied, looking sideways.

"You're either Leon or you're not!" I said, feeling a mix of frustration and curiosity.

"Whether I am or not, how does that concern you?" he asked.

"I was in school with a guy who looked exactly like you, named Leon. I thought you might be him," I explained, trying to suppress my irritation.

"Does that mean every Leon you see was your classmate?" he retorted before returning to his newspaper. I felt embarrassed and angry. If his surname was Silvester, then he was indeed my schoolmate.

As we approached the registration desk, I glimpsed through the glass window that his name was Leonardo Silvester, and he was from my former school.

Fast forward to five years later, my friend asked me to help interview applicants for various jobs in his company. Among them was Leonardo Silvester.

When he entered the office and saw me, he suddenly stopped in his tracks, lost for words. I enjoyed asking him about his background, hobbies, and goals.

When the interview was over, he mumbled, "I know I have failed this interview."

Smiling enigmatically, I responded, "Well, well, well... it will depend."

Despite our past encounter, I didn't see the need to deny him the job opportunity. He had the qualifications, and I believed two wrongs don't make a right. I proceeded to forward his name as one of the successful candidates.

Many times, when Leonardo was at my friend's office, he would be asked to ring and pass business information to me. He once confided that his hardest moment was when his employer asked him to come to my office. Eventually, Leonardo dropped his pride and apologized for denying that he ever knew me as his former classmate.

As the saying goes, the world is indeed very small.

Time to Reflect:

How would you have responded if you or someone you know were called upon to help someone who had denied knowing you?

What lesson can you instil in your children, colleagues, or siblings about doing good to all to help others thrive?

Chapter Seventeen: *Don't Compare Yourself to Others*

Just when I thought that I would never lack money simply because I was in England, I was surprised to find myself in a bad financial position in what was then the fourth greatest nation on earth. I was behind on payments, and my credit report was very poor.

One Saturday morning, I went to withdraw my last £10 from the bank. While standing in the queue, I noticed an old friend in the corner expertly handling bundles of bank notes in several A4 envelopes, making me wonder if we were living in the same country with the same opportunities. He had businesses both locally and in London, while I had a decently paid day job but still struggled to make ends meet. This is one reason why I love the idea of being in business.

After being served, my friend spotted me and was happy to see me. He suggested we meet at a nearby restaurant to catch up. I agreed, even though I only had £10 in my pocket and needed to do some shopping. We met as planned and started chatting.

"Hi James, nice to see you! How time flies! It's been a year since we last met!" he said with a broad smile.

"Yeah, Jakes, it's great to see you. You left our company without saying goodbye... How's everything going?" I asked.

"I'm glad I formed a company. It's doing well, in my opinion. My sales for the last financial year were slightly over £5M," he responded.

"What? £5M in sales?" I asked in astonishment.

"Of course. All you need is a good team, good connections, and a bit of luck. I call it standing on the shoulders of giants!" he replied, before continuing, "You have what it takes. You can start a similar business. I don't mind showing you the ropes. If you can gather at least £50K to start, I can subcontract some business to you. You must transform your thinking and see life beyond your day job. Otherwise, you'll always have just enough to survive but not to invest. You'll be stuck in a rat race, and with time you'll be too old with nothing to show. This is the time to do things differently!"

I couldn't believe such words of wisdom were coming from someone who had once asked me for money. If I only had £10, where would I get £50K for starting capital? The meeting ended with me telling Jakes I would get in touch, which was obviously a lie. In truth, I wasn't ready to face him again.

As I drove away, I wondered where I went wrong financially. Was my brain inferior to Jakes'? Did someone bewitch me? How could I be in England and live a dog's life?

The more I questioned myself, the more I admired Jakes' business acumen and lifestyle. If I were him, I thought, I would invest in real estate globally and live off passive income. I would travel the world and dine in five-star hotels.

A year after our meeting, I heard Jakes had been diagnosed with a terminal disease. I drove to London to see him and was heartbroken to find that the once robust, handsome, and confident man I met at the bank was now a pale shadow of himself. Sadly, at his end-of-life period he could no longer recognize me. Soon after, he passed away and was buried.

When we met, I envied Jakes, not knowing he had a terminal disease despite his financial success. What if we had exchanged lives? Never wish to be anyone else. You are unique, created one out of millions. In life, some people are brighter, richer, or more attractive. It's foolish to imitate them or wish to be like them. In the privacy of their bedrooms, they have their own troubles.

Time to Reflect:

Have you ever wished you could walk in the shoes of someone you admired? Consider if you would be willing to take on their challenges, successes and the journey in-between to get to where they are now.

If you were offered the chance to live 'a day in the life of XYZ' what would you do differently now with the benefit of hindsight?

Note to self: Enjoy life now that you have the chance. Live each day as if it's your last because, one day, it will be!

Chapter Eighteen: Listen To Your Gut Feeling

I was having drinks with friends in the city when a middle-aged man approached me and greeted me by my nickname. For him to call me that, he must have been from my village and known me well. I couldn't remember him despite repeatedly looking at him.

"Hi James, how have you been? I left your village when you were a young boy! How time flies! Just the other day you were going to school smelling of smoke," he said jokingly.

"The smoke part is true, but to me, you're a stranger. Where did we meet?" I asked.

"I used to visit your village a long time ago. Your brothers and I used to swim in the river near your grandmother's place. Do you know the old man who lived next to the river that bordered your farm? That was my uncle," he laughed. "My name is Desmond."

I had brothers his age, but I still couldn't remember him. Eventually, I 'agreed' he was a long-lost friend.

"Only mountains do not meet! I've always wanted to see you. There's a business opportunity we can pursue. I have government connections, but I need someone to front me. If we join hands, the sky's the limit, James!" he said.

No doubt, my best subject is business, so I ordered more drinks to hear more about his ideas. The more we drank, the more grandiose his business plans sounded. When I asked what kind of business he was involved in, he said he would tell me in private.

When he excused himself to go to the toilet, I followed him out of curiosity. When I asked what he was doing, he gestured with his hands that he was in special branch police, so he couldn't share such sensitive information in public.

After midnight, as I was about to leave, he asked for a ride home. He said it was just a two-mile deviation south from my route home. I agreed and we set off. On the way, I kept asking about his work, but he was evasive.

"Nobody in intelligence will ever discuss their work. It's against the law," he said. "But if you want proof, look at this," he said, revealing a small pistol from his coat pocket.

We were supposed to take Jogoo Road, but Desmond asked me to follow Mombasa Road as he needed to check something.

"You know we are on duty 24/7. When we reach City Cabanas, just wait for me for five minutes," he said. Since he was planning a multi-million business deal, (or so he said), I was willing to wait as long as needed.

Life Lessons for the Wise:

When he returned to the car, he smelled strongly of liquor. The pungent odor made me uncomfortable, so I drove quickly, keen to drop him off. The area around Pipeline and Embakasi was barren land, dark and isolated.

When I stopped, I thought Desmond would get out immediately, but surprisingly, he lingered and talked endlessly, delaying for over two hours.

Suddenly, my pager beeped. In those days mobile phones were uncommon, and pagers were rarer. The message from my brother read, *TAKE YOUR CAR TO THE NEAREST POLICE STATION IMMEDIATELY AND WAIT! AVOID...*

Avoid what?! I wondered. Noticing my distraction, Desmond excused himself and went outside for a smoke. He stayed just within sight, smoking for five, ten, fifteen minutes. As he started walking back to the car, a sudden fear gripped me. My instincts screamed *DANGER*!

Immediately I started the engine and drove off as fast as my car would go. Through the rearview mirror I observed him trying to wave me down but ignored him.

Later, I discovered that Desmond was a highway robber, not a special branch officer. His pistol was for his criminal activities. My brother, knowing about Desmond's activities, had paged me to save my life.

In retrospect, I had a narrow escape. Moreover, Desmond's prolonged time outside the car was suspicious.

Time to Reflect:

Always listen to your gut feeling, your sixth sense. Your subconscious mind often knows more than you realize.

Before engaging in any relationship or business venture, listen to your instincts. If you have a bad feeling, reconsider. Most importantly, ask God to guide you.

Do not be wise in your own eyes;
Fear the Lord and depart from evil.
— Proverbs 3:7

Chapter Nineteen: *Do Not Lose Hope*

I once informed my friend in Africa that I was going on holiday with my family. After mentioning the airline we were using, he asked if I wasn't scared of flying with them.

"Of all the airlines, is this the one you chose? Don't you know one of their Boeing 777s crashed in the Mediterranean Sea last month, killing everyone on board?" he asked.

Since I hadn't heard about the crash, I reassured him, saying it didn't mean our plane would crash. He sighed heavily, clearly concerned.

"Well, if it does crash, you'll make a good meal for the sharks," he joked. Not wishing to dwell on the flight's safety, I left everything to God.

A week before our trip, I bought my dream car, a luxury I was certain to miss dearly, along with my office, house and other earthly belongings.

Before our departure, I withdrew some cash in hard currency to use on holiday. I put the money in an envelope and hid it under the driver's seat of my car. When the taxi arrived to take us to the airport, I asked my son to retrieve the cash from the car.

We arrived at Heathrow Airport, and the plane took off. We were scheduled to have a stopover in an African city before continuing our journey.

While flying over Greece, I noticed my son repeatedly checking his briefcase and pockets. I asked what was wrong, and he told me he forgot to get the cash from the car and even left the car unlocked with the keys inside.

"What?! You did what?! Are you mad?!" I exclaimed, aghast.

"Dad, I'm so sorry. Words can't express how sorry I am," he said, close to tears.

"Now what are we going to do when we arrive in Africa? What about money for accommodation, food, and getting around? 'Sorry' isn't legal tender!" I said angrily. My son had never seen me so upset, so he fell silent. As we flew, I continuously reminded him of the mess and shame he'd caused us.

"All I can say is that I'm sorry. I wish I could rewind the clock," he said softly.

"Tell it to the birds!" I responded in frustration.

I imagined how disappointed the apartment owner would be when we arrived without money. I feared my new car would be stolen, with £4K disappearing thanks to my son's careless mistake. Observing my foul mood, my son pretended to sleep. I, too, decided to sleep but asked my wife and daughter to wake me up for meals.

The plane cruised smoothly until we hit turbulence. Startled, I looked out the window and saw the plane struggling in the turbulent air. My son also woke up and asked what was happening.

"Just a bit of turbulence, it's normal. It'll pass," I assured him. With that, he went back to sleep.

However, the turbulence worsened. Everyone was quiet, hoping for the best. Twenty minutes passed, then thirty, with no improvement. My son woke again, suggesting the problem was more serious.

As I assured him again, I was deeply worried, especially remembering the crash my friend had mentioned. My hope dwindled when the flight captain instructed the staff to stop serving immediately. When my wife and children looked at me for reassurance, I told them everything would be okay, though my confidence was shaken.

In that moment of fear, I prayed silently for our safety, asking God to protect us and everyone on board.

"God, if we come out of this, we'll be happy and praise Your Name. I'll never fear anything again. In You I trust and believe, in Jesus' Name. Amen."

After fifteen minutes of intense turbulence, the plane finally leveled out and continued cruising normally. Relief washed over everyone. Thank God, we made it!

At 4:30 am, we landed in the African capital city then boarded another plane to Nairobi.

I apologized to my son for my harsh words, assuring him that leaving the money behind wasn't a big deal. After all, any problem solvable with money wasn't really a problem.

During the turbulence, I realized that if we had crashed, it wouldn't matter if I had left £4K under the car seat or owned a brand-new car.

Upon arrival at our destination, I called my brother, who retrieved the money from the car and secured it. My car and money were safe. We appreciated the emergency funds our credit cards afforded us to enjoy our memorable holiday.

Life is fleeting, and material possessions are meaningless when facing mortality. For those who take life too seriously, remember that no situation is permanent. Life has its ups and downs which we must accept. Sometimes, God brings challenges to sharpen us.

That experience taught me not to take life as if I'm a permanent resident in this world. I now correct my children gently, without anger. I thank God for their lives and cherish my role as their father.

Time to Reflect:

Sometimes we worry needlessly. This is often due to how we're raised to see everything as an emergency.

Stop worrying and start living. Focus on what works in your life.

Do not lose hope because life is not an emergency.

Chapter Twenty: *Look At the Bigger Picture*

After buying a better car, I wanted to sell my older car. Keeping two cars meant paying for insurance, road tax, and maintenance for both, which was an unnecessary financial burden. With an extra car sitting in my driveway, I was also losing money I desperately needed.

Two months after advertising the car sale through friends and social media, there were no takers. The thought of selling it as scrap was disheartening since the car was worth £3,000.

One evening, a friend who knew a car dealer called me. The dealer was willing to pay £3,500 for the car. I couldn't believe my luck! After the payment, the buyer took the logbook but didn't change the ownership details until he sold the car. This meant that if the car was caught speeding, the fine would come to me unless I proved that I had sold it. Desperate for the money, I didn't insist on a formal agreement for the change of ownership.

Then, two weeks later, I started receiving parking tickets from the London council for a car I no longer possessed. There was one week where I got a ticket every day, each costing £130.00! After contacting various London councils, some cancelled the tickets after I provided evidence of my innocence.

However, others required more concrete evidence, which I didn't have. It was time-consuming and stressful, involving numerous calls, emails, and endless trips to the post office. Despite my efforts, I couldn't clear my name completely, and eventually gave up writing to them. It wasn't worth the hassle for something I hadn't done.

I was then asked to pay the ticket plus a 50% late fee. Failure to pay within seven days would result in a county court judgment (CCJ) against me. This would severely impact my credit report, making it difficult to get credit for the next six years. If I did get credit, it would come with high-interest rates due to my tarnished creditworthiness.

In the business world, maintaining a good credit report is crucial. Cash flow is king, and bank support is essential. Rather than risk my credit history over a £200 fine, I decided to pay, even though I had ample evidence that I wasn't the car owner at the time the penalty was issued.

Time to Reflect:

Sometimes, even when you know you're right, it's better to accept being 'wrong' for peace of mind. Not every battle is worth fighting, especially if it can harm your well-being or relationships.

My failure to ensure that the car's new owner changed the logbook's name immediately turned out to be a big mistake in the long run.

You are your best manager and should know which battles are worth fighting. There are times to raise your voice and times to avoid drama. Always look at the bigger picture.

Chapter Twenty-One: *A Blessing in Disguise*

One day, my client informed me of a new job he wanted us to undertake. The job required a security guard to visit the site at regular intervals within a 24-hour period. As the job was due to start in three days, I needed to find a security guard quickly.

The guard's responsibility was to walk around the fence, check for any intrusions, and make a report. I advertised for the job, but people were reluctant to apply because it wasn't a continuous assignment. Driving fifty miles from my home to the site wasn't economically viable, and other big security companies were eager to take the contract, putting my other contracts at risk. I was also willing to pay more than usual to satisfy my client.

As I pondered my options, I noticed a man of colour with a small girl in school uniform walking towards me. I hoped he might be interested in the job or know someone who was. When he passed my car, I asked if we could chat, and he agreed.

"Hi mate. My name is James, and I oversee security for this site. I'm looking for a security guard," I told him.

"I'm Geoffrey, the neighbour to your site," he replied with an emotionless face.

"Nice to meet you, Geoffrey. What exactly do you do?" I asked, hoping he was looking for work.

"What a stupid question! You just met me and you're asking what I do? What do you want me to do?" he responded.

"I'm wondering if we can help each other. I desperately need someone to take care of the site. Since you're the neighbour, could you spare a few hours to walk around and check for intrusions?" I explained.

"That's fine. I've been looking for work since February," he replied with interest.

I was overjoyed to have found someone to help me avoid the inconvenience of constant travel. Later, he asked about the pay. I offered £35 per visit, as the perimeter patrol would take less than ten minutes. The minimum wage at the time was £8.50 per hour.

"What! Only £35 per visit? What do you take me for?" he asked dismissively.

"But if you do three patrols, you'll have £105 to your credit," I said.

"You talk about £105 as if it's a fortune that can give me life after death?" he scoffed.

I assured him we could discuss and come to an agreement. However, he gestured to his kid and left without taking my contact or the job offer.

My next option was to undertake the job myself and find ways to mitigate costs. After that, I rented a room near the site and did the job. Eventually, I readvertised and got five applicants, picking the best one.

By good fortune, another local client approached me about offering security services for their premises, requiring four guards. I employed the remaining four applicants for this new contract.

I've come to believe that when you pray for something that is of good report, God blesses it. I could have refused the first client's offer, considering nobody wanted the job requiring site visits at intervals. Despite feeling disappointed when the neighbour refused the job, my stepping in to save the day turned out to be a blessing in disguise.

Time to Reflect:

Sometimes, setbacks are opportunities in disguise. When faced with challenges, don't be quick to give up.

Instead, look for creative solutions and trust that something better may come along.

What seems like a problem might be the path to your greatest success.

Chapter Twenty-Two: By Their Fruits

After a long, hectic day at work, I found myself alone in the office as everyone else had already headed home. Instead of rushing to the bus station and dealing with the long queues, I decided to stay back for another hour, hoping to avoid the crowded commute. As the quiet minutes ticked by, I grew restless and decided to take a stroll down the corridor to pass the time.

As I approached the far end of the hallway, I heard my name being called. It was Oliver, one of our senior managers. "James! James! Nice to see you! You must have just returned from your annual leave, right? I stopped by your office earlier and told your colleagues I had exciting news for you from one of our clients. I was hoping to catch up with you."

Surprised, I responded, "Oliver, that's news to me! I just got back today, and no one mentioned you were looking for me."

"Well, no harm done," he said with a grin. "Our client is launching a new property at one of the five-star hotels in the city, and you're invited. The launch starts at 8:00 pm, but there's a cocktail party beforehand at 6:00 pm. I suggest we head over there now."

Since I had never been to a cocktail party before, the thought of sitting with our three company directors and senior managers made me anxious.

This was only my fifth month with the company, and I was still figuring out how to navigate being around the higher-ups. I tried to come up with a hundred reasons why I shouldn't go, but Oliver wasn't having any of it.

"You're not going to turn into a reptile just because you attend a launch," he said, chuckling at my nervousness.

Realizing there was no way to avoid it, I reluctantly agreed, and we headed to the nearby hotel. On our way there, my mind was consumed with the fear of not fitting in, wondering how my village manners would hold up in such a setting.

Upon arrival, we were greeted like royalty. Oliver, noticing my discomfort, strove to keep me engaged, introducing me to important people who readily handed me their business cards. Unfortunately, I didn't have any cards of my own to give them. As we mingled during the cocktail party, I tried to blend in, but struggled to connect with my seniors, despite Oliver's best efforts.

Then, a thought crossed my mind—maybe a few beers would help. Beer has a way of boosting false confidence, and I desperately needed some. It worked like a charm. Soon, I found myself deep in conversation with our Managing Director about ways to reduce operational costs.

Oliver kept giving me warning winks, but I pretended not to notice. As the night progressed, we enjoyed speeches, exchanged ideas, and the atmosphere became more relaxed. When raffle tickets were sold, I bought one, just to blend in. To my astonishment, my name was called as one of the winners!

I couldn't believe my luck—I had won a weekend for two at a five-star hotel on the coast, complete with a bottle of wine upon arrival and a VIP Gold Membership card valid for three years. This card entitled me to stay at any of their hotels for free on three weekends over the next year.

Ironically, Oliver didn't win anything, but he still congratulated me, as did the directors. It was a night to remember, and I couldn't stop staring at my gold card and vouchers with pride.

Since Oliver lived close to my house, he offered to drive me home. On the way, we chatted about the party and the guests; he even suggested that we could visit the hotel together with our spouses. He also seemed to enjoy my continued gratitude for making my night unforgettable.

"James, if you want to rise in this company, always roll with senior staff like Oliver," he advised as we cruised through the night.

When we arrived at my house, I bid him goodbye, and he promised to take me to lunch the next day to discuss how I could make the most of my VIP membership.

Life Lessons for the Wise:

The next morning, as soon as I got to my office, my phone rang. To my surprise, it was the Managing Director's secretary, informing me that the Director wanted to see me. A cold chill ran down my spine. Was I in trouble for something I had done the previous night? I wondered.

Summoning my courage, I entered the Managing Director's office where he greeted me warmly and offered me a seat.

He thanked me for attending the event, even though I wasn't in the Marketing Department, and expressed his appreciation for how I had entertained his colleagues during the launch. I thanked him in return, but my mind was racing, trying to figure out the real reason for the meeting.

What happened next floored me. The Managing Director showed me an email from Oliver that had been copied to all the directors. In it, Oliver suggested that I should be stripped of my VIP Gold Membership because I wasn't in the Marketing Department. He also criticized my interaction with the directors, claiming I was drunk and disorderly, and that I should face disciplinary action.

Stunned, I asked the Director what he thought of the email. Laughing it off, he replied, "Forget about the email. You're a star, James, a real jewel. I'm happy to have someone like you in our company!"

Relieved to know that the Managing Director thought so highly of me, I returned to my office and tried to focus on my work. But no matter how hard I tried, I couldn't shake the disappointment.

How could Oliver, of all people, stab me in the back like that? What was his motive? I decided to confront him. I called Oliver and thanked him for his company the previous night, relaying how much I enjoyed it and how happy the directors were.

After congratulating me again on winning the raffle prize, he continued, "If you play your cards right, that membership can catapult you to a level you've never dreamed of. Lucky you!"

"Mr Oliver, thanks for the opportunity yesterday. But as you congratulate me, could you also advise me on how to avoid disciplinary measures for being drunk and disorderly during the launch?" I asked. The moment he heard my request, he hung up.

It was clear to me that my colleague was jealous of my newfound success. Through this experience, I learned that office politics is a reality we must all navigate.

Time to Reflect:

Colleagues are often comfortable with you when you're on the same level, but once you start to progress, they can become uncomfortable.

When the situation demands that you stoop low, just stoop low.

When the situation demands that you stoop low, just stoop low.
— Lawrence Carlos

Chapter Twenty-Three: *Cheap is Expensive*

Jon worked as a payroll manager at the company, while Moses was a messenger. Whenever Moses had payroll issues, he consulted Jon. However, Moses had an odd habit of looking sideways or at the ceiling when talking to Jon, his hands and face sweating profusely.

"Moses, it's hard to help you if you don't look at me," Jon said one day.

"I don't have to look at you. You're not a lady! Who do you think you are? You're just an employee like me, and if management decides to sack you, they can!" Moses retorted.

"What kind of man doesn't look at another man when talking to him?" Jon asked.

"You're questioning my manhood? Let's have a fight and you'll see what kind of man I am," Moses responded angrily.

"You're right, Moses. I agree with you one hundred percent," Jon said, trying to deescalate.

One Friday afternoon, Moses came to Jon's office. Jon asked him to sit down for a chat.

"What! You want me to sit with you? I wish I could avoid your office! You're such a bad colleague to work with!" Moses exclaimed.

"Moses, I understand. Maybe you're right, maybe you're wrong, but we can't work with this tension," Jon said.

"So, what do you want to discuss, 'Professor' Jon?" Moses asked sarcastically.

"I'm sorry if I've ever offended you. I ask for your forgiveness," Jon said sincerely.

"You should have said that a long time ago. You always talk to me like a kid, and I don't like it! Anyway, apologies accepted," Moses said, shaking Jon's hand.

The following Monday, Moses arrived at Jon's office with a smile, looking Jon in the eye. Jon smiled back but avoided jokes to prevent any misinterpretation. Moses needed Jon to approve a staff loan to pay rent.

After talking for about fifteen minutes, Moses revealed that his family had been made landless. "My dad used to own a hundred acres near the city, but now we're landless," he said, tears welling in his eyes.

"Your dad owned a hundred acres...and now you're landless? Did he sell it?" Jon asked.

"No, he never sold it. We woke up one day to find people fencing our land with signs saying, 'PRIVATE PROPERTY, TRESPASSERS WILL BE PROSECUTED,'" explained Moses in a distressed voice.

"Moses, I still don't understand," Jon said.

"Within an hour, bulldozers demolished all our houses," Moses continued.

"Then what happened?" Jon asked.

"We had to put up temporary shelters along the road. We went from owning a hundred acres worth a lot of money to having nothing in one day," Moses said.

"Did your dad have a title deed?" Jon asked.

"Yes, a genuine title deed. We inherited the land from our grandfather," Moses replied.

"Please, take me through what happened. This doesn't sound real," Jon encouraged Moses.

"Well, my dad was very humble and valued friendships. He was illiterate but befriended everyone, including Jacob, a prominent butcher in town. Jacob often let his goats graze on our land, and my dad got free meat in return. Dad trusted Jacob completely. One day, Jacob asked dad to sign some papers, saying they were for a bank loan application that needed two signatures."

He continued: "My dad trusted Jacob and signed without reading them. To make matters worse, he did not tell anyone in the family about the incident. Over time, dad asked Jacob to find another place for his livestock because we wanted to start large-scale farming. Jacob then accused dad of being mean and stopped talking to him."

"Two months later, dad's cousin asked why he sold the land to Jacob. Dad laughed it off, thinking it was a joke. Without warning, we were greatly surprised one morning when bulldozers arrived and started demolishing our houses. That is when we learned that my dad had unknowingly signed over the land to Jacob. We moved from one government office to another trying to get our land back, but nobody helped."

"My dad became severely depressed and now he can't look after himself. My mom has dementia, and I pay rent for both my parents and my family. We went from being wealthy to paupers because of my dad's misplaced trust," Moses concluded with a deep sigh.

Time to Reflect:

Take a closer look at the people you let into your life. Some people are better loved from a distance because they are not genuine friends.

Before you sign anything, think twice because you might be signing away your future.

Chapter Twenty-Four: *Blame Yourself*

During a particularly harsh winter across Europe, with schools closed and travel advisories in place, I decided to escape the cold and travel to Africa for a holiday. The hot African sun beckoned, the perfect destination.

Before leaving, I bought presents for friends at my local mall. On my way out, I spotted a watch priced at £1,095.56. It was stunning—golden, shiny, and changed colours. Despite its high pricetag, I decided to buy the watch.

Departing from Heathrow Airport, we had a stopover at Ataturk International Airport in Istanbul, Turkey, before continuing to Nairobi. During the flight, I admired my new watch frequently, feeling proud of my purchase.

Seated between two middle-aged Turkish men on our first leg of the journey, I couldn't help but notice one of them eyeing my watch enviously.

"Nice watch! Must have cost you a fortune!" he said.

"Oh, thanks! It did, but it's worth enjoying life's pleasures," I replied.

"Be careful when wearing it in some places; someone might snatch it," he warned.

Life Lessons for the Wise:

After about three hours, the watch felt heavy, so I placed it under the small table in front of my seat.

Exhausted from lack of sleep, I dozed off, struggling even to eat when food was served. As we entered Turkish airspace, I remembered a college friend named Kerem from Turkey. He was the only white man in our class and often struggled with English. Despite his differences, he was fearless, even arguing with police if needed.

When we landed, I eagerly disembarked and made my way to the immigration desks. After the long flight, I gratefully stretched my legs in the vast Istanbul International Airport. After grabbing a coffee to refresh myself, I went to wash my face and hands. Just then I realized my watch was missing!

Panic set in. I recalled leaving it under the makeshift table on the plane. On rushing back towards the plane's exit, the door was locked. An airport staff member directed me to a desk a mile away to report my missing watch.

Frantically, I sprinted across the airport, only to be told I was at the wrong desk. This happened twice more, each time increasing my frustration and desperation. When I finally reached the right desk, the officer, irritated by my repeated visits, reluctantly directed me to the information desk in the adjacent room.

There, I filled out forms, sensing deep down that recovering my watch was unlikely. Preparing myself for disappointment, I tried to find peace.

As the time for my connecting flight to Nairobi approached, I was convinced the two men beside me on the plane had taken my watch. Settling into my seat, I decided to read a novel. Reaching inside my briefcase, I felt something metallic. To my astonishment, it was my watch!

Surprisingly, I had forgotten that I had transferred it into my bag before going to the toilet on the plane. Immense relief and joy washed over me.

Reflecting on the situation, I realized my own carelessness caused the panic. Moreover, I unfairly blamed others and endured unnecessary stress.

Time to Reflect:

When things go wrong, it's crucial to first examine our own actions.

Often, we are the architects of our misfortunes, attracting them through our thoughts and behaviours.

Avoid blaming others and seek to establish the truth of the matter.

Chapter Twenty-Five: *Nothing Is Worth Dying For*

After a delicious lunch at the hotel, my family and I decided to go for an afternoon game drive in the expansive National Park. The warm weather was a welcome change from the harsh winter cold in Europe.

We marvelled at the diverse wildlife: lions, rhinos, giraffes, antelopes, elephants—all roaming freely. Baboons and monkeys kept watch from elevated spots, wary of predators. Antelopes, ever vigilant, grazed with caution, always aware of lurking lions.

At around 5:30 pm, we spotted a lion hiding in a bush, eyeing an unsuspecting gazelle grazing nearby. We watched quietly, feeling an urge to warn the gazelle of the impending danger. In a swift, powerful leap, the lion attacked and began its meal. My children, who had never seen even a chicken being slaughtered, were horrified by the sight.

After driving a long distance, we arrived at a stunning waterfall in the middle of the park. Our driver guide explained that the river's source was in the nearby mountains. The sight of water plunging several feet before continuing its course was breathtaking.

Half an hour later, we noticed other tourists heading back to the hotel. We decided to follow suit, aware that the wild animals could pose a threat as night fell. The thought of becoming prey was unsettling.

We had to travel about a hundred metres further into the park before reversing because of the narrow roads. Our hearts pounded as we drove in the dark, quiet park. My wife and children were clearly uncomfortable, knowing that we were risking our lives with every passing minute.

Barely thirty metres in, we spotted a man in a green coat sitting alone, reading a newspaper in an open space. My children nearly screamed in disbelief. Who in their right mind would be out there at that hour, surrounded by wild animals?

I asked our driver to approach him and offer a lift. The man laughed at my concern.

"Thank you, but I'm okay! I work here," he responded.

"But how do you get back to camp with wild animals around? Do you have a weapon?" I asked.

"A weapon? I just have a stick, a normal stick!" he replied.

"Aren't you scared to be here at this hour?" I pressed.

"Scared of what? I'm a real man, not a cockroach!" he retorted. Despite my repeated offers, he refused our help, insisting he would walk. He seemed completely at ease, focused on his crossword puzzle.

As we left, I couldn't help but think he was tempting fate. No matter how experienced he was, he was courting death. It would only take one hungry animal to end his life.

Reflecting on this encounter, I realized how often we put ourselves in danger, while fully aware of the risks. No job, no matter the pay, is worth risking your life. If a job poses a threat to your health or well-being, think twice before continuing. The man in the park lived by sheer favour.

Time to Reflect:

Whatever you do, prioritize your happiness and well-being.

A job causing constant stress isn't worth it.

Living life to the fullest means avoiding unnecessary risks. Remember, *nothing is worth dying for*.

> Life is really simple, but we insist on making it complicated.
> - Confucius

Chapter Twenty-Six: *Love in Those Days*

A Child's Definition of 'Love'

In the tiny village where I was born and raised, *Valentine's Day* did not exist. Villagers didn't know or care about who Valentine was or what his customs were.

This doesn't mean village people lacked feelings of love. They had love but did not demonstrate it openly.

In my tribe, *love* began at dancing ceremonies. If a man was interested in a girl, he would approach her and express his desire to marry and have children with her. If the girl was interested, she'd tell him to inform her parents. The young man would then tell his parents, who would either approve or disapprove. If they approved, they would send friends to investigate the girl's family, checking for family curses, work ethics, and behaviour.

As a young boy, my first brush with a concept like *Valentine's Day* came through my cousin Judy and a worker from the village polytechnic. Judy was the village darling, a brilliant student who got into a prestigious high school. Everyone told us to study hard like Judy.

When she came home for the holidays, Judy would take me for walks that always ended at the village polytechnic. There, she'd meet a young man who wore platform shoes.

They would hug and kiss briefly, stopping when they saw me watching. Whenever I asked Judy if she was serious about kissing, she would swear it was just a peck on the cheek. Thereafter we would go into the young man's house where he served us delicious food usually reserved for Christmas. While we ate, I noticed he couldn't take his eyes off Judy.

Sometimes, Judy would send me to a distant shop to buy biscuits and a Fanta. Though a nearer shop existed, I didn't mind running the extra miles for the treat. One day, after returning from the shop, I found the door locked and heard Judy's voice inside, occasionally letting out sharp screams. Panicking, I banged on the door, shouting at the man to stop hurting her. The screams stopped, and Judy came out, reassuring me and promising that next time we'd bring our big dog, Simba, to scare him. Naively, I believed her.

It was getting dark, and we had to go home. To my surprise, the man who had just made Judy scream was now holding her hand as he walked us back. Instead of being angry, Judy was squeezing his hand, telling him she loved him. When I asked her what love meant, she said it was eating biscuits with a Fanta.

"So, I made love this afternoon in the shopping centre?" I innocently asked.

"Of course, yes!" she replied.

That night, I excitedly told my brothers about my 'lovemaking' adventure.

They struggled to conceal their laughter, especially after recounting Judy's screams and the bad man from the polytechnic.

Time to Interact

Reflect: Have you ever misunderstood something as a child that seemed funny when you got older? Share your story with friends or family.

Discuss: What customs or traditions around love and relationships exist in your culture? How do they compare to the story?

Imagine: If you were in the young boy's shoes, how would you have reacted? Would you have been as brave? What might you have done differently?

Write: Create a short story about a humorous or innocent misunderstanding you had as a child. Share it with someone you trust.

Remember, love and relationships have always been part of human culture, even if expressed differently across times and places. Embrace the humour and lessons from these tales of old!

Chapter Twenty-Seven: *Not All That Glitters Is Gold*

Our plane landed at Budapest International Airport from UK's Luton Airport at 9 am GMT. After a smooth immigration process, everyone went their separate ways.

Taking a cab to my hotel I was immediately captivated by Budapest's beauty. Budapest is made up of two cities, Buda and Pest, separated by the expansive Danube River. The river stretches 2,800 kilometres and flows through ten countries, including Germany and Austria.

My hotel was on the Buda side, right by the Danube. My top-floor room had a stunning view of both cities. After a couple of hours alone in my room, I decided to explore the city on foot.

Walking across the bridge was exhilarating, though a bit nerve-wracking. I emerged on the other side near the Houses of Parliament, reputed to be the third-largest parliament building in the world at that time.

After five hours of walking, I noticed something strange: I hadn't seen another person of colour. It felt eerie to be in a city where no one looked like me. As I strolled by, locals frequently asked to take photos with me, which I agreed to.

As the sun began to set, I decided to head back to the hotel. Within five minutes, I saw two black men running towards me. Before I could say hello, they both hugged me warmly, beaming with joy.

"My brother, how are you? Nice to see you, brother! Welcome to Budapest!" they exclaimed in unison. I was taken aback by their enthusiasm and friendliness.

"I'm James from East Africa. Where are you from?" I asked, though I could tell they were from West Africa.

"This is Martin, and I am Sam. We are both from West Africa. Together with you, we are brothers!" Sam said.

We were thrilled to meet each other and talked a lot. I asked why they had come to Eastern Europe instead of Western Europe. They explained that they were seeking greener pastures, but life had been tough. They had married local women, which posed challenges due to cultural differences.

"My brother, please help us get out of this place! Jobs are scarce, and it's hard to support our families in Africa. Please, take us with you to London, we beg you," Sam pleaded, tears streaming down his face.

While I couldn't take them to London, I offered to help them find jobs if their paperwork was in order. They looked hungry, so I suggested we get something to eat at a nearby restaurant. They were overjoyed by the offer. In the end, I gave £20 to each and asked them to contact me via email. Unfortunately, I never heard from them again.

Time to Reflect:

Martin and Sam's story is not unique. Many people leave their home countries in search of better opportunities, only to find life abroad exceedingly difficult.

Not all that glitters is gold.

Chapter Twenty-Eight: *Mistaken Identity Abroad*

Finding My Place in a New Land

When I first arrived in England, I found myself in an old city that seemed like a piece of paradise. Its enchanting beauty boasted sunrises that painted the sky in golden hues and sunsets that disappeared into distant horizons. The summer greenery and rolling hills added to the charm, making it a place I could see myself retiring in.

Exploring the city, I marvelled at the thousand-year-old cathedral and ancient Roman wall that still stood tall. One of the most fascinating sights was a river that flowed in the opposite direction, especially at night!

However, my initial excitement was tempered by a sense of isolation. I was the only person of colour in this beautiful but strange city. The TV shows airing at 9 pm were nothing I would feel comfortable watching with my children, which added to my sense of alienation.

With no one to talk to, I sought solace in bookshops. One day, I entered a bookshop with only one staff member at the counter. She almost froze upon seeing me. I tried to ease her nerves with a friendly "hello," but she responded with a faint greeting, visibly shaking.

As I browsed the shelves, she watched my every move, her eyes darting between me and the CCTV camera.

After spending two months in the city, I decided to eat at a local restaurant. While enjoying my meal, I noticed a group of school children who seemed to have just returned from a trip. One girl in particular kept staring at me. Whenever I glanced her way, our eyes would meet, and she would continue to stare.

She had finished her burger but not her chips. As her teacher announced it was time to leave, she approached me with her uneaten chips and asked if I wanted them. *Me?* I politely declined, smiled, and thanked her for the offer.

As she boarded the school bus, I pondered why she thought I might want her leftover food, even though I was smartly dressed. This made me reflect on the images many people in the West have of Africa—a continent they often associate with hunger, despair, and disease. The woman in the bookshop likely thought I was a thief because she assumed I came from a place of scarcity.

When I told my children I would take them to Africa for the first time, they cried and begged me not to take them to a place they believed was filled with danger and deprivation. It took a lot of effort to convince them that the Africa they saw on television was not the whole truth. If my own children had such a low opinion of Africa, what about that girl who offered me her food that was meant for the bin?

The negative perceptions of Africa run deep. As a person of colour, it's essential to strive for excellence and add personal value so we are relevant in Western society.

We cannot afford to be average because the West has no place for an average person of colour. We must therefore go the extra mile to succeed and make a significant impact.

Time to Reflect:

In his book *The Science of Getting Rich*, Wallace D. Wattles states that being poor is abnormal considering the abundance that surrounds us.

Resources are plentiful and sufficient for everyone.

If we do not stand out, we remain invisible and are ignored by the world, despite our talents.

Let us determine to rise above the ground to be seen and respected, and ensure we are not mistaken as people destined for the lowest rungs of society.

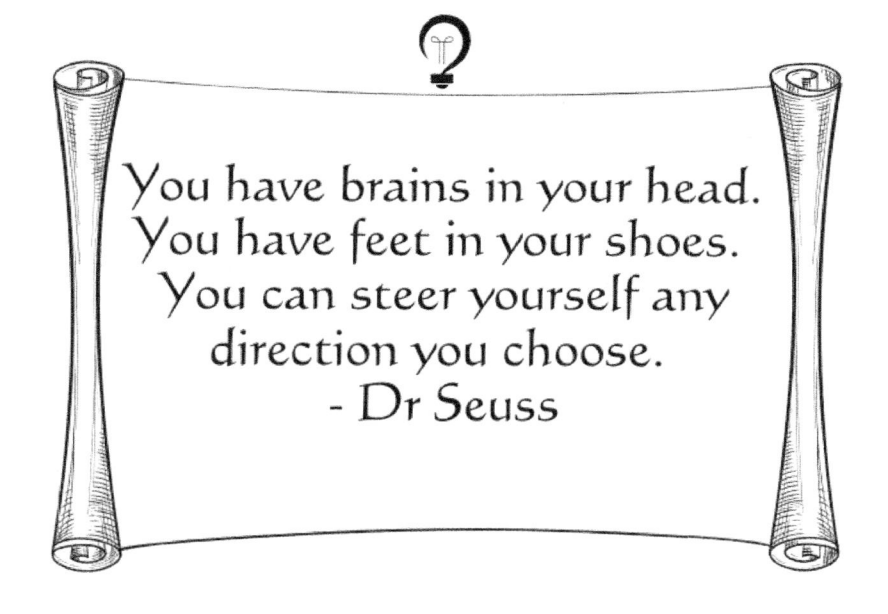

You have brains in your head.
You have feet in your shoes.
You can steer yourself any
direction you choose.
- Dr Seuss

Chapter Twenty-Nine: A Father's Regret

A call to action...

Have you ever thought about the deep impact your actions can have on another person's life? Discover the consequences of neglect.

Years ago, in Budapest, I met a man from Kenya. We became fast friends and, one night, he shared a heartbreaking story. He had a son, born when he and the boy's mother were both students in Russia. Unable to provide for them, he left his pregnant girlfriend and returned to Kenya to find work.

Over the years, he received letters and photos of his son but never responded. His son grew up, moved to Budapest, and built a life for himself. Tragically, he lost his life from a car accident. In his final days, the son had pleaded with his father to attend his funeral, a plea that went unanswered until it was too late.

The man's story was a heavy weight, pressing down on the quiet room. I felt a deep sorrow for this man consumed by regret. His words reminded me of life's fragile nature and the irrevocable consequences of our choices.

We talked long into the night, the conversation shifting from his pain to a broader exploration of fatherhood.

The bereaved father spoke of the heavy cultural pressures on men, the expectation to provide materially rather than emotionally. He shared stories of friends who were similarly absent from their children's lives, caught in a cycle of neglect.

As dawn approached, a sense of peace settled over him. Perhaps it was the catharsis of sharing his story, or maybe it was simply the passage of time. Whatever the reason, there was a newfound resolve in his eyes.

"I want to make a difference," he said quietly. "I want to use my story to help other men understand the importance of being there for their children."

In that moment, I saw a spark ignite within him, a determination to turn his pain into purpose. And as the first rays of sunlight touched the city, I knew that this was just the beginning of his journey.

The following days were a blur of planning and action for the Kenyan man. He reached out to local community groups, men's organizations, and even schools. His story was raw, his vulnerability striking. People listened intently, hearts heavy with empathy. He began speaking at events, sharing his experience with a candour that was both heartbreaking and inspiring.

His heartfelt message was simple: **Be present. Be involved. Be a father**. He urged men to break free from societal expectations and prioritize their relationships with their children.

He spoke of the importance of emotional connection and being more than just a provider. Slowly but surely, a community began to form around him. Men who had been on the fence about their role as fathers started to re-evaluate their priorities. Young fathers sought him out for advice, eager to avoid past mistakes. Those who had already lost touch with their children found hope in his story, lighting the darkness of their regret.

His story resonated far beyond the borders of Budapest. As news outlets picked up on his message, soon he was a familiar media face. The response was overwhelming. Letters poured in, each one attesting to the collective ache of parental longing. Men confessed their regrets as women shared their struggles of raising children alone.

But with the growing acclaim came a new set of challenges. The emotional toll of reliving his pain was immense. Critics emerged, questioning his motives and accusing him of exploiting his personal tragedy. There were days when the weight of it all seemed unbearable.

Yet, through the storm, he found solace in the countless lives he was touching. Every message of hope, every story of reconciliation, further fuelled his determination. He resiliently established a foundation to provide support services for absent fathers, offering counselling, mentorship, and financial assistance.

His journey was far from over. While the road ahead was filled with uncertainties, he was no longer alone.

He had become a symbol of hope, demonstrating the power of vulnerability and the enduring spirit of the human heart.

Time to Reflect:

Do you have any regrets for an action you did or failed to do that had negative consequences? You can find a way to help others avoid the pain.

Start by forgiving yourself.

Then make a difference.

Chapter Thirty: *Aim High and Seize Opportunities*

A Story of Resilience and Success.

One day, I attended a business networking meeting featuring a key speaker, an influential figure in the world of business. I had read all his books but had never met him in person, and I was eager to see him face to face.

The speaker began by introducing himself and sharing his story. He had joined the Air Force as a jet fighter pilot deployed to the Middle East. When he left for duty, his wife was two months pregnant. The harsh Middle East conditions meant he had to stay there for over three years, often waking up in the middle of the night, crying, unsure if he would ever see his wife and child again. Many of his colleagues had died in the line of duty, and he feared the same fate. His constant prayer was to return home to see his newborn baby.

By a stroke of favour, his annual leave request was approved. He planned to surprise his wife and child with a secret two-week holiday in Switzerland. However, just as they were packing to leave, he received a call from his boss.

They were short of jet fighter pilots, and he was ordered to report back immediately. Shocked and frustrated, he considered lashing out but instead chose to resign.

This decision left him jobless, with no income and mounting bills. His credit rating suffered, and with a young family to support, he turned to his innate skills. He had always excelled in people skills, so he approached property owners, offering to be their caretaker. Initially, it was tough, but his trustworthiness earned him referrals. Within six months, he had a significant number of clients.

Within a year, his estate agency became his full-time job, allowing him to employ people from his town. Two years later, he expanded to other regions, opening branches across the UK. He soon managed a portfolio of hundreds of properties with over a thousand tenants in one city.

He concluded his speech with powerful advice: "Opportunities surround us everywhere. Anyone who knows how to use a phone has a chance to succeed. Just as a tiny seed grows into a mighty fig tree, we too should flourish day by day." He emphasized the importance of setting goals that benefit society and don't harm us or our loved ones.

He also advised detaching from the outcome of our goals. In a world of abundance, being too rigid is like a big oak tree that gets uprooted in a storm, while reeds bend and stand straight again when the storm passes.

This flexibility and resilience are key to achieving success and overcoming life's challenges.

Time to Reflect:

Have you taken an honest look at your goals recently? Where do you need to adjust? Ask God to align you to your purpose-driven life.

Chapter Thirty-One: *Don't Waste Your Chance*

It took me exactly two hours to fly from London's Luton Airport to Budapest International Airport in Hungary. I was scheduled to spend one week with a potential client and then head back to England after two weeks.

After clearing immigration, I found myself waiting for my luggage along with the rest of the passengers. Among the crowd, I noticed a young Black man, around twenty years old, carrying a small bag. He looked lost and confused. Incidentally, we were the only two people of color in the luggage area. Just before we exited the airport, I turned to him to introduce myself.

"Hello, sir," I said.

"Oh, nice to meet you. I am Tobias," he said, shaking my hand.

"Nice to meet you, too. My name is James," I replied, extending my hand.

As we waited for cabs outside, I asked if he had arranged transportation to his hotel. After a brief pause, he mentioned that his host had given him a number to call once he arrived.

Since my client had dispatched a driver to pick me up, I offered Tobias a lift to the city centre, and he agreed.

We drove past the Pest side of the city before crossing over to the Buda side. Budapest is made up of two cities, Buda and Pest, separated by the Danube River, which spans 2,800 kilometres and passes through ten countries, including Germany and Austria.

I sat in the front with the driver while Tobias sat in the back. Occasionally, I glanced at him through the rearview mirror and saw him mesmerized by the beauty of Budapest, especially the magnificent Houses of Parliament by the Danube.

It took the driver twenty minutes to get us to the hotel. My client was scheduled to meet me the following day, so I had some time. I suggested that Tobias call his host to see if she was nearby. He tried calling a few times without success. On the fourth attempt, the driver offered to call her using his phone. Luckily, she answered.

"Hello, is this Faith?" asked the driver.

"Yes, it is! Who are you, and how did you get my number?" she enquired.

"I'm with a gentleman named Tobias who wants to speak with you," the driver explained.

"Who on earth is Tobias?" she asked.

"He's a young man from the airport," the driver replied, handing the phone to Tobias.

Tobias and Faith exchanged casual greetings. From their conversation, it was clear they had never met, but their talk centred on one person. Faith said she would come for him later, as she was two hundred miles away from Budapest.

I decided to stay with Tobias at the hotel, despite him being a stranger. I checked in and invited him to my room. We had lunch, which he ate hungrily, and then relaxed on the sofas with some soft drinks.

"So, where in Africa are you from?" I asked casually.

"I'm from West Africa," he replied.

"What brings you to Hungary?" I continued.

"I've come to see someone," he said.

"What kind of 'someone'?" I pressed.

"Just someone I saw in a photo. She's a stranger to me," he answered vaguely.

"You flew all the way from West Africa to Budapest to see someone you've never met? She's not your girlfriend or even your pen pal. What's the story?" I asked, growing impatient.

He revealed it was his first time out of his country and on an airplane. When I asked how much money he had, he said he only had $20.

I excused myself to use the bathroom. When I returned, I found Tobias looking at a photo of a middle-aged woman.

He started to cry, and when he saw me, he quickly put the photo away.

"What's the matter, Tobias?" I asked.

"Nothing," he said.

"But you're crying," I pointed out.

"I'm just sad," he replied, heading to the bathroom.

While he was away, I called Faith again. After several attempts, she answered.

"Are you ever going to leave me alone?" she snapped.

"I just want you to come and get your visitor," I told her.

"If he's consuming oxygen around you, why don't you switch it off?" she retorted.

"Faith, let's be reasonable. This young man is distressed. He's crying. Please come for him before it's too late," I pleaded.

"Before he cries again, ask him if he's going to pay the money his mum owes me," she demanded.

"I don't understand the correlation between your debt and coming to get him. Why can't his mother come for him?" I asked.

"Stop pretending you don't know! Just tell him he needs to pay me $200," she responded without compassion.

"Why don't you trace his mother? He's just a twenty-year-old student," I argued.

"I know you know the story, but you won't fool me. I'm smarter than you think!" she said before hanging up.

When Tobias returned, I told him Faith was on her way to the hotel. He looked astonished.

"Don't bother about paying that debt Faith mentioned," I assured him.

"What debt? By whom?" he asked.

"Tobias, stop pretending you don't know what I'm talking about. You're not to blame for your mum's deeds," I said.

"You mean you know about my mum? he asked, revealing that he had come to Budapest to see his mother, who had lived there most of her life.

"Does that mean you were possibly born here?" I asked.

"No, I was born in West Africa. My mother gave birth to me, then left me with my grandmother who raised me. She never visited me or her parents, even when she married a Hungarian and moved to Europe. She completely forgot about us," he said, tears flowing down his cheeks.

"You have a chance to meet her face to face now. She has a lot to answer for," I told him.

"I thought Faith told you everything!" he exclaimed.

"Not that bit," I replied.

"I've never seen my mum alive, and I never will. She died last week from ovarian cancer. Her funeral is the day after tomorrow," he said.

"You mean she's dead?" I asked in disbelief.

"Yes, she passed away. Faith and her friends arranged for my airfare so I could attend her funeral. That's why I'm here. I came to say goodbye to the mother I never knew. She wasted her chance to see me alive. How I wish I could have met her, even for a minute, to tell her that despite everything, she was my mother, and I loved her unconditionally. Now, it's too late. I hope she finds peace in the next world," he concluded with a sigh.

When Faith finally arrived, I paid her the $200 she demanded from Tobias. I believed his story after seeing his passport and witnessing him and Faith at the cemetery during the funeral.

Time to Reflect:

When you wake up each day, remember it's a golden chance given to you. You can use it to be nasty or to be a blessing.

If you have children you've abandoned, today is the day to reconnect with them. Talk to their mother and rise above any past grievances.

Life is too short.

Chapter Thirty-Two: *The Power of Your Tongue*

I was sitting in a restaurant when I spotted a familiar face I hadn't seen in years. It was Dominic, or Dom for short. When he saw me, he came over with a big smile and joined me at my table. I was just as thrilled to see him because he always had a great sense of humour. After exchanging greetings, we started chatting.

"Nice to see you, Dom! Finally, after eight years in England, we meet again. Where have you been, you son of a gun?" I asked jovially.

"I've been on paternity leave. My twins are doing well," he replied.

"Congratulations! You must be the first man to give birth to twins with hairy tongues!" I joked.

"Actually, I've been in jail for the last five years. I regret all those lost years," he said, his tone turning serious.

Dom had already served a two-year jail term before coming to Europe. I had hoped he would have turned his life around, but old habits die hard. I started thinking that he wasn't the kind of person I wanted in my circle of friends.

I preferred to surround myself with people who had a good moral compass, which Dom seemed to lack. In awkward silence I pondered his character.

After a few minutes, Dom told me he had been looking for me because he needed my help. He thought I could connect him to a relative of mine who had government connections. He was convinced my relative could help him get government contracts.

"I want to be rich! I'm sick of living a dog's life in Europe. The only way is up!" he said.

While I could have connected him to my relative, I wasn't willing to vouch for someone with a criminal record.

"Sure, Dom. I feel your pain. You didn't come to Europe to serve jail sentences but to build a better life. When my relative visits Europe again, I'll make sure you meet him and talk about government contracts," I offered.

"Thank you! You're a godsend. I see riches flowing to me because of you! When I'm filthy rich, I'll testify that my success started with you!" he exclaimed. In my mind however, I still saw him as a jailbird, not a future millionaire. As soon as I got to my car I deleted the phone number he gave me.

Two years later, I ran into Dom again at the same restaurant. He joined us, giving firm handshakes all around. To my surprise, he pulled me aside to thank me for the advice I had given him during our last meeting.

"Thanks for listening to me and encouraging me to change my mindset. You told me to see myself as a winner and speak positive things into existence. I didn't have good connections, but I had a phone and a mouth. I started a limited company and approached businesspeople for contracts. My business is taking off, and my turnover last year was over £1M!" he confidently shared.

"Well done! That's impressive. How much are you worth now?" I curiously asked.

"In the last quarter, I paid £50k in VAT. Since our last meeting, with a transformed mindset, I'm on the right path. There's no turning back. I'll always speak positively because what I confess with my tongue becomes reality," he concluded.

Looking at Dom's life, I was amazed by his transformation. He had started seeing himself as a winner, not a victim. Through his positive mindset, he began attracting good things into his life.

Time to Reflect:

Life and death are in the power of the tongue. What we confess is what we become.

How are you using your mindset to create new, empowering realities in your life?

> When you undervalue what you do, the world will undervalue who you are.
> — Oprah Winfrey

Chapter Thirty-Three: *Take a Closer Look*

One Saturday afternoon, while sat in my client's office, I noticed a van moving at a snail's pace about a kilometre away. It passed slowly and then returned just as slowly, with the driver's head sticking out of the window.

Curious, I left the office and went to the road to ask the driver what he was looking for. When I stopped him, he got out of the van.

"Hello, sir. You seem lost. Are you looking for something?" I asked.

"Not really," he replied. "I was just bored at home and decided to look for some company. Living alone can be really boring."

The stranger was exceptionally tall, thin, and emaciated. His eyes seemed deeply sunken, which struck me as very unusual.

"Do you have a family?" I asked conversationally.

"Thank God I've never had one, and I never will. I have no interest, he said, extending his hand. By the way, my name is Ahab."

Ahab told me his mother, a single mom, gave him up for adoption at birth because she couldn't take care of him.

Moreover, throughout his sixty years, he had never seen or heard from his mother. After the first family that adopted him gave up on him when he turned two, he was sent to another family. Sadly, the foster children wouldn't play with him because they saw him as an outsider.

I asked him how he survived without parental love from the start.

"It wasn't easy. I had to train hard to defend myself. That was the only way to survive; otherwise, bullies would have made my life miserable," he replied. He mentioned having earned a black belt in Tae Kwon Do to protect himself. He couldn't imagine having children of his own because he didn't want them to experience the cruelty he endured. Furthermore, women reminded him of his mother who abandoned him. With each explanation his voice became increasingly hysterical.

"If you met your mom today, what would you tell her?" I wondered.

"I'd tell her to stay away from me. What kind of mother abandons her child?" he asked indignantly.

"How about forgiving her? Maybe she couldn't take care of you," I suggested.

"As you make your bed, so you lie on it!" he exclaimed.

The more we talked, the more I liked him. He started visiting my workplace on weekends, and we discussed various societal issues.

Impressed by his mastery of martial arts, I asked him to show me some techniques. We agreed to start training the following Sunday.

He began with the basics and gradually moved on to tougher techniques. During one session, he suddenly grabbed and locked my neck with his elbow, and lifted me off the ground with full force. Desperately gasping for breath, I urgently gestured for him to stop, but instead he tightened his grip until I lost consciousness. When I later regained consciousness, he was towering over me and spitting on my face.

"Go back to Zimbabwe! Go back to Africa, you son of a gun!" he shouted angrily.

After regaining my breath, I told him to leave immediately, or I'd call the police.

As he walked away, he reminded me, "You asked me to train you. You knew the risk. I'm not your girlfriend, you fool!"

"I didn't ask you to kill me, you idiot!" I retorted.

With that he jumped into his van and sped off.

The next day, a neighbour walking his dog pulled me aside and asked if I was friends with Ahab. I responded that we were just acquaintances.

"A piece of advice," he began. "You've just started the end of your journey on earth if you keep entertaining him."

With that he walked away without explaining further, leaving me with something to think about.

That terrifying experience helped me realize I had made a huge mistake by trusting a stranger too quickly. I should have got to know him better before asking him to train me in martial arts.

In real life, it's not uncommon to befriend people who later see you as a tool for their gain. They might involve you in various schemes, making you their financial slave. Even in church, it's wise to discern if it's genuinely Bible-based or just a business enterprise. Be cautious, or you risk being brainwashed and controlled.

Back to Ahab... Only God knows what he intended when he made me lose consciousness. If he wanted to kill me, he could have. If he wanted to inject me with poison, I was at his mercy. What if I hadn't trusted him? Could I have avoided this ordeal?

Time to Reflect:

When you start something driven by emotions, take a moment to evaluate if it's worth it. If your subconscious mind tells you to stop, listen to the voice of wisdom.

Choices have consequences.

Take a closer look; you never know.

Chapter Thirty-Four: *Stop Being Your Own Enemy*

Years ago, when I was job hunting, I experienced a particularly challenging year. Promises of employment consistently fell through. One well-to-do person kept telling me, "Let's give next week a break, come the week after." This went on for a whole year. I began to think of that year as exceptionally bad, and since it ended in an odd number, I convinced myself that every year ending in an odd number would be difficult for me.

Sure enough, in the following years, all the years that ended in odd numbers proved tough, especially in relationships and finances. My worst moment came when I was made redundant; that year also ended with an odd number.

Even after moving to Europe, I held onto this negative belief. Unsurprisingly, significant hardships continued to manifest in the odd-numbered years. It seemed like whatever I accumulated in an even-numbered year was wiped out by the challenges of the odd-numbered year. To crown this undesirable trend, I was made redundant again in another odd-numbered year.

The following year, which ended with an even number, I managed to acquire a lovely home to rent out.

However, the following year, my tenant faced financial difficulties and couldn't pay rent. The house remained vacant for months and caused me to lose significant income.

As the new odd-numbered year approached, I came across a clip titled *The Strangest Secret* by Earl Nightingale. He revealed that what a person believes, they become. Any thought, good or bad, will manifest because nature always executes what the mind believes. Wise people understand that nature takes us seriously; it will function as you tell it, and no thought in our minds stays rent-free.

Determined to change my mindset, I told myself that the upcoming odd-numbered year would be a new beginning. That year, I got my first breakthrough in business. As an added blessing, our company expanded into another European country, and my life began to improve significantly. I even had the opportunity to vacation in many countries around the world.

This experience taught me that old thoughts and beliefs must be shed. Your thoughts and beliefs determine whether you are poor or successful. Everyone was born to flourish, not to live a mediocre life. Change your thoughts, and you change your life! Carry yourself as the most favoured person alive.

Believe that *nothing happens against you but **for** you*.

Time to Reflect:

Have tremendous faith in God and let Him be your guide. Believe that you live in a world of abundance and that you have the capacity to receive all the good things the world can offer.

While God guides and protects you, do yourself a favour: *stop being your own enemy!*

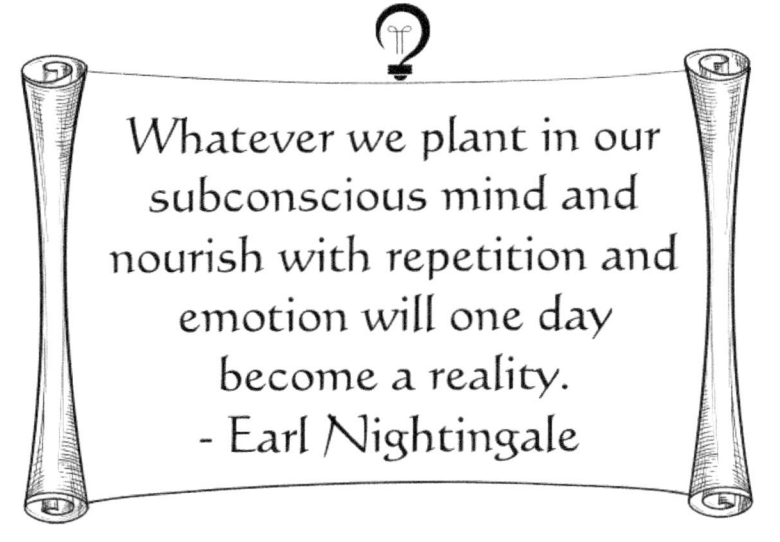

Whatever we plant in our subconscious mind and nourish with repetition and emotion will one day become a reality.
- Earl Nightingale

Chapter Thirty-Five: *Rise Above Your Thinking*

Every day I wake up in good health, I recognize it as a privilege. Regardless of whether I'm going through challenging times or not, I always consider myself incredibly blessed. If you don't believe in blessings, you'll always find it hard to achieve what others seem to get easily.

Every morning, as I drive to work, I take time to pray for at least three people who come to mind. These could be people from my primary school, high school, college, past and present workplaces, friends, enemies, relatives, or even the motorist ahead of me. I ask God to grant them good health and success in all their endeavours.

The other day, as I was driving to work, I thought of my friend John and prayed for him. While praying, I reminisced about our interactions and what John was like as a classmate. John was always the top student from Form One to Form Four. What amazed everyone was that he didn't study as hard as the rest of us.

While the rest of us immersed our heads in our books late into the night, John would go to bed by 9 pm, yet he always scored the highest marks in exams.

Because of his academic prowess, he became the school administration's favourite.

In our high school, the Head Boy role was a coveted position. The Head Boy wore a black suit, white shirt, and black tie provided by the school. He also had the principal's ear, making him almost like a teacher. While other boys slept in the dormitory, the Head Boy had his own small one-bedroom house attached to the dormitory. Due to his popularity and leadership skills, John was chosen as the Head Boy, a title everyone desired.

John was enthusiastic about joining a prestigious high school for his A-Levels. This school was the best in the nation, consistently producing top results. During a provincial ball game, the principal of this prestigious school saw John playing volleyball and was impressed. He approached John and encouraged him to choose his school for A-Levels.

Unlike the rest of us, uncertain about our future after O-Level exams, John knew he was heading to his dream school. True to form, when the final exams came out, as the top-performing student, John easily secured his place at the prestigious high school.

At his new school, John's academic brilliance earned him the Head Boy title once again. When the exams were out, he was the top student with maximum points. We often joked that he wrote the marking scheme during the exams!

John went on to university, earning a First-Class Honors degree and becoming the chairperson of his course association. After university, he received many job offers but turned them down, waiting for his passion in a particular profession. He soon joined a corporate job and was promoted quickly. Within five years, he became a billionaire, investing heavily in various sectors.

Looking back, John seemed incredibly lucky. He only needed to mention something, and it would come to him. I've often wondered what trick John used to be so fortunate, and I've realized it all starts with our minds. The picture we have of ourselves is the picture we show the world, and the world treats us accordingly.

A British Prime Minister Benjamin Disraeli once said, "You cannot rise above what you are thinking, so you must think big."

Time to Reflect:

Above all, strive to have peace of mind. Be at peace with yourself and the world to attract good fortune. Otherwise, you'll create friction in your life, and good fortune will always evade you.

You attract what you respect; conversely, what you disrespect moves away from you.

Chapter Thirty-Six: *Remain Calm in Every Situation*

Recently while driving to work, I realized I was going to arrive an hour early. To kill some time, I slowed down. My route involved a narrow road where overtaking was tough, and I soon noticed a dark blue van tailgating me. The driver was a middle-aged man with dreadlocks and thick glasses.

As we approached the main road, traffic slowed us down. I could see the van driver getting increasingly agitated. He was wiping sweat off his face, shaking his head, pulling his hair, and banging the steering wheel.

Signalling to take the next left exit toward my workplace I further reduced my speed as an ambulance approached and moved to the extreme left to let it pass. The van driver parked behind me, looking at his watch and hitting his steering wheel in frustration. When I resumed driving, he pulled up close to my right.

Curious about his behaviour, I glanced at him and rolled down my window as he muttered something.

"You stupid man, where did you learn how to drive? You almost made me cause an accident!" he shouted angrily.

Initially, I didn't realize he was talking to me. When I asked if he was addressing me, he exploded.

"Of course, I am talking to you! Who taught you how to drive? This is England, and you're driving at a snail's pace! You idiot! Go back to the forest you came from!"

He spewed curses recklessly, which I found strangely amusing. After rolling up my window, I plugged my ears with my fingers. Meanwhile the irate driver continued his tirade, banging his dashboard and throwing things around his car. When he was done, he sped off, weaving through traffic and overtaking cars recklessly.

Instead of responding in kind and using my machismo, I wisely chose to engage my brains. The best way to handle an insult is to let it go in one ear and out the other. I could have escalated the situation to a physical confrontation, but that would have damaged my reputation and integrity.

Time to Reflect:

Whatever the situation, remain calm.

If confronted by an aggressor, don't stand face to face.

Mentally disarm the aggressor by stepping back and staying at a 45-degree angle.

Rise above mediocrity by refusing to engage in pointless arguments.

Finally, *don't catch a falling knife; remain calm always because life is not a rehearsal.*

Chapter Thirty-Seven: *Seize the Opportunity*

Not too long ago, I had to head into the city for some engagements, and instead of driving myself, I decided to take the train. My children kindly offered to drive me to the station, with my daughter taking the wheel.

As I sat in the back seat, jotting down some notes for the day, it struck me that this was the first time I'd ever sat in the back seat since buying the car. In fact, none of my children had ever driven me before. It was a new experience.

As we neared the station, my daughter turned to me and asked, "Dad, does it feel weird sitting in the back while we're up front?"

"So long as you're driving safely and we're all okay, that's all that matters to me," I replied.

But before I could finish my thought, my son chimed in with a playful grin, "Dad, the back seat is where you belong now. It's our time!"

Looking up from my notes in surprise, I asked, "Are you serious?" I then put the papers back into my briefcase.

"Dad, I'm just joking!" he laughed, knowing I'd never take offense to something like that.

Soon enough, we reached the train station, and I watched as my children drove off, disappearing down the road. Moments later, the train arrived, and I settled in for the journey to the city. As the train wound its way through the countryside, my son's words echoed in my mind: "Dad, the back seat is where you belong now. This is our time!"

On reflection, maybe he was right. After all, my kids are no longer the little ones I brought to Europe years ago. The days of waking them up, bathing them, making their breakfast, and walking them to school are long gone. I used to love taking them to the shop to buy little treats like chocolates and biscuits. They believed every word I said, even the harmless fibs, simply because I was their dad.

I remember flying with them, and as soon as we were in the sky, they'd ask me if this was where God lived. How I miss those days! But now, they're just memories.

Now, imagine if I hadn't been there for them when they were young. If, as teenagers, they asked me where I was and why I left, what could I possibly say? I would have missed out on watching them grow, and there's no way to turn back the clock. Life is full of moments that come only once. If you let them slip through your fingers, they're gone for good.

Think back to when you were a child, sitting around the dinner table with your family, your mom serving food before you all went to bed.

As time passed, everyone left home to live their own lives. Those moments are behind you now, and they won't come back.

Time to Reflect:

Whatever you're doing right now, do it with care and attention.

Don't miss your chance—seize the opportunity. As the old Latin saying goes, *Carpe diem*!

> In depth of winter, I finally learned that within me there lay an invisible summer.
> — Albert Camus

Chapter Thirty-Eight: *The Power of Giving*

When the co-pilot announced that we were leaving the Mediterranean Sea and entering European airspace, I couldn't help but smile. Finally, I was on my way to the land of plenty, a place I'd heard was overflowing with opportunities—a land where money practically fell from the sky, or so I thought.

As the plane circled over London, I was captivated by the beauty below. The city was so neat and well-arranged, it felt like I was gazing down at a slice of Heaven. If this wasn't Heaven, then Heaven must be something beyond human comprehension.

When I landed, I was relieved to find that people were incredibly friendly, eager to show me the ropes of surviving in the Western world. My main goal from day one was to land a job—specifically, an office job like the one I had back in Africa.

But to my dismay, that office job was nowhere to be found. With the help of friends, I went from one employment agency to another, only to be offered what they called 'dirty' jobs. These gruelling labour-intensive factory jobs were a far cry from the intellectual computer work I was used to.

Some assignments required working in freezing conditions; the harsh winter outside felt no different from stepping into a giant freezer.

During my first break at work, I found myself questioning if relocating to the West was the right decision. Where were all the riches and opportunities everyone back home had talked about? The truth is life in the West isn't always a walk in the park. The factory work was so tough that I couldn't bring myself to do it every day, leaving me with less than £100 a week in wages.

Being a devout Christian, I started attending a church in East London led by a West African middle-aged pastor. Interestingly, my friends noted that he resembled me. I was eager for God's guidance in this new land, especially when it came to improving my financial situation. With a young family to support, I couldn't afford to see them go hungry. The sooner my finances improved, the more confident I would feel.

After one service, the pastor announced that the church was facing financial difficulties and asked if anyone would contribute £5,000 to support God's work. I was stunned. £5,000?

To my amazement, several hands shot up, including one from a fellow person of colour. I wondered how much someone like that must be worth to so confidently pledge such a large sum.

I silently prayed to God, expressing my willingness to give, but admitting that my wallet was empty. After church, I devised a plan: I would start writing small cheques to the church, whatever I could afford, and pray for God to increase it. If He did, I would raise the amount the following week.

Over time, I began to realize that the church leadership seemed more interested in our money than in teaching the gospel. They even asked my two-year-old son to contribute, claiming that since he received child benefits, part of it belonged to the church. That was the last straw. My family eventually left that church and prayed for God to lead us to a Bible-based church that was less focused on money.

We found a spiritual home in a Catholic church, where our children were already attending school, and the teachings weren't as commercialized. I had asked God to bless me financially so I could support His work, and every Sunday, I started giving a £5 cheque, which was all I could afford.

"God, if You give me more, I'll contribute £10," I frequently prayed. While the months went by with no visible change in my financial situation, my faith endured. Then, things started to improve. With time I was able to afford £15, then £20, £30—wow! Eventually, my tithe and offerings grew to £50, £100, even £200 a week by cheque.

This growth wasn't because I was particularly skilled at making money; I realized it was because God had blessed me with a little and trusted me with more. The key is to start giving, even if it's just a small amount, to a good religious organization that isn't all about business. If you can only afford a single coin, give that coin and ask God to increase it. If you pray for something good, God, in His mercy, will provide.

Later, our parish launched a project, and they asked members to contribute. The maximum contribution was £5,000, but any amount was welcome. To my surprise, the bishop personally requested that I contribute £5,000, which I gladly did.

Time to Reflect:

A fig tree begins with a tiny seed. Over time, through God's mysterious ways, that seed grows and flourishes into a mighty tree.

Life works the same way—you were born to flourish because that's how nature is designed.

Chapter Thirty-Nine: The Eleventh Hour

One holiday, I decided to visit a piece of land I had bought while living abroad. I'd been told it hadn't been developed, despite being in a prime location. But when I arrived, I was shocked to see that 98% of the area had been built up, and children were using my plot as their playground.

After parking my car, I walked around and took it all in. The kids played happily, completely unaware that the land belonged to me. Before long, two men pulled up in a salon car and approached me.

"Hello, sir. I'm Martin, and this is my brother Bob. We live around here," one of them said, extending his hand.

"I'm James, just enjoying the weather!" I replied, trying to gauge what they were up to.

"Are you looking to buy land? We could sell you this entire plot if you're interested," Martin said, smiling.

I was stunned. This was my land, and here they were trying to sell it to me! They even mentioned that the owner, supposedly living in America, had asked them to handle the sale. That's when I knew that I was dealing with con men. I played along, telling them the price was too high for me. After some back-and-forth, they eventually left, but not before giving me their contact information in case I changed my mind.

Realizing the land was at risk, I had to act quickly. I decided to fence it off and build a small, semi-permanent house with a toilet so someone could stay there as a caretaker. I asked around for someone who might need free accommodation in exchange for looking after the land. Luckily, a neighbour knew of an elderly man who was nearly homeless.

When the house was ready three days later, I met the man. His belongings in sacks, he was accompanied by four children who looked painfully thin and poorly dressed. Despite being in his sixties, the man himself was also frail.

"I guess you're the person my friend mentioned," I started.

"Yes, that's me. I can't thank you enough," he replied softly.

"My name's James, and I own this land," I told him.

"You're an angel. You've come into my life at the eleventh hour, just when I needed help the most. I haven't paid rent in three months, and the landlord was about to evict us. We had nowhere to go, so you can imagine my relief when I heard you needed a caretaker," he said, tears welling up in his eyes.

I noticed he kept referring to the children as his grandchildren, so I asked, "Where are their parents?"

He explained that the children's mother, his daughter, was an alcoholic. She had been absent for over a year, leaving him to care for her kids. The last time he saw her, she was so drunk she couldn't even recognize her own children. The next day, she left and never returned.

Weeks later, my holiday ended, and I returned to England. On my next trip back, I decided to check in on the man and the kids. To my surprise, I arrived to find the place empty. After waiting for hours with no sign of them, I eventually asked a neighbour if he'd seen them that day.

He invited me into his home and told me the elderly man had been admitted in hospital for the past week.

"Hospital? What happened? Was he sick?" I asked, growing concerned.

"It was a terrible misfortune," the neighbour began. "The grandfather was on his way to a nearby coffee plantation for work. He had to cross a river, but the bridge was made of just a few logs laid across. After heavy rain, the river flooded, and it became dangerous to cross. Since he needed the money to feed his grandchildren, he took the risk. As soon as he stepped onto the logs however, the raging waters swept him away."

The neighbour went on to describe how the man was carried downstream, out of sight. It seemed hopeless as people searched for him. Miraculously, the grandfather managed to grab onto a tree by the riverbank. Although he was covered by branches and debris, he could see them searching nearby. In desperation, he prayed, asking God to protect him for the sake of his grandchildren.

Finally, some of the branches moved, making him visible. Just as people were beginning to lose hope, one man spotted him and swam over to rescue him.

They managed to pull him to safety and even raised money to get him to the hospital.

Time to Reflect:

There are moments in life when we face challenges that only divine intervention can resolve.

The grandfather's story reminds us that sometimes, when we're at our lowest, God hears our cries and grants us a second chance.

When these moments of grace come, we must seize them and cherish them, for they may never come again.

Chapter Forty: *Tomorrow Will Come*

In my new department, I had a colleague who brought lots of fun to the workplace that it made everything feel lighter and more enjoyable. It made me wonder why more managers don't make their offices places where people can laugh and work at the same time.

Part of our job involved sending invoices and collecting debts. To ensure transparency, we had only one credit notebook in use at any given time; keeping it secure was essential. Since we dealt in foreign currencies, the amounts could be significant, sometimes reaching hundreds of thousands of dollars, yen, or pounds.

One day, I made a mistake by forgetting to sign out the last person who had used the credit notebook. When a Head of Department asked me for it, I couldn't produce it because I wasn't sure who had taken it. At first, I assured him I'd find it, but as time passed—ten, fifteen, twenty minutes—I still hadn't located it, and he was becoming increasingly frustrated. Eventually, he called me into his office.

When I arrived, he was pacing the room, talking to the Financial Director.

"Sir, I don't know what to do with him! Our Barcelona office needs this credit note to release $200,000, and I've been asking for it since yesterday. Why did you put James in this position? We need to get rid of people like him!"

His secretary then informed him of my presence. As I entered, he smilingly greeted me with a firm handshake.

"James, don't worry. What's a credit note, really? Take your time, man! If you worry, you die. If you don't worry, you also die. Pack your troubles and smile! Smile! Smile!" he said. Since I had just overheard him trying to get me fired, there wasn't much to smile about. I left his office feeling crushed.

Back at my desk, I saw an email from the same manager. He was complaining about the missing credit note, stressing that over $200k was at risk of being delayed by our Barcelona office. To make matters worse, he had even copied in all the departmental Heads and their deputies, essentially putting my job on the line.

Thankfully, shortly after another manager called to confirm what had happened to the missing credit note. Apparently, when I had briefly stepped out of my office earlier, he had popped in and taken the credit note from my desk, to complete a transaction with our American office. In his hurry to secure the deal, he forgot to sign it out. Although he apologized, the damage was already done.

I felt ashamed, guilty, and worried about possibly losing my job over it. Understandably, my heart was still heavy when I returned the notebook to the Head of Department.

Years later, I relocated to Europe. During a holiday in Lloret de Mar, Barcelona, I decided to visit the office that had almost cost me my job.

As my family and I were about to enter, guess who I ran into? The very HOD who had tried to get me fired! Ironically, he was still working for our former employer, while I was just a tourist in the city.

He seemed genuinely surprised but friendly. We agreed to have lunch with my family, but even then, I pretended to be happy to see him. That unfortunate incident flashed into my mind as I tried to erase the memory of his mistreatment.

Who would have thought we'd cross paths again in Barcelona, of all places? You never know what tomorrow holds, so it's important to treat people with dignity and respect.

Time to Reflect:

No weapon formed against you shall prosper. Remember, your colleagues are just that—colleagues, not necessarily friends.

If your heart is clean, God will put your enemies to shame. Life is full of all kinds of people, both good and bad.

When you encounter enemies, thank God for revealing them, but love them from a distance.

The real test of honor isn't how you die; it's how you live.
— Michael J. Fox

Conclusion

Thanks for reading the book **Life Lessons for the Wise**. My hope is that you have learned a life lesson or two and gained some nuggets you will share with others.

When I was growing up, most of the women of my mother's age were not educated so they would trust me with reading and interpreting the letters they were receiving from their spouses. Some of the letters had very angry tones and there was no way I would pronounce some words in the letter. Instead, I chose to avoid the words and inform them what the sender meant. In this way, I helped to reduce the tension that would have built up if I told the receiver exactly what was written. If we apply wisdom to tackle issues, we will live very happy lives.

May these lessons guide your communication, decision making, attitudes and life to create harmonious relationships that empower, inspire and transform many lives in your growing sphere of influence.

Would you honour me with a quick favour? Please take a minute to share this book's **ISBN: 9798339147848** with your contacts because we are our brother's keeper.

Finally, follow me on Amazon and Facebook to be notified when new stories are released for you.

Thank you and God richly bless you.

Lawrence Carlos

About the Author

Mr Lawrence Carlos lives in Northampton, United Kingdom. He is married to Mrs Mary Carlos and together, they have two children, Michelle and Herman. Lawrence is an avid businessman.

Lawrence has always had a passion for helping others. His influence on helping people comes from *Hermann Gmeiner* (1919-1986), founder of the *SOS Children's villages*. No wonder he named his son Herman, after he was born. If we cared for humanity the way Hermann Gmeiner did, the world would be a better place.

In his spare time, Lawrence likes to motivate people through talks and writing, enabling them to enjoy their God-given time in this world. The book **Life Lessons for the Wise** has many lessons the author holds dear. We are the way we are because of our past thoughts and beliefs.

After reading the book, the author is confident that the reader will consider the wise investment of time to be worthwhile.

Follow the author to be notified when he releases more impactful stories in the **Whispers from the World** series.

Share this book's ISBN: 9798339147848

Connect: https://www.facebook.com/LCARLOSMANMAN/

Printed in Great Britain
by Amazon